Making Waves

Integrating Coastal Conservation and Development

Katrina Brown

Emma L Tompkins

W Neil Adger

Earthscan Publications Ltd
London • Sterling, VA

First published in the UK and USA in 2002
by Earthscan Publications Ltd

ISBN: 1 85383 912 4 paperback
      1 85383 915 9 hardback

Typesetting by PCS Mapping & DTP, Gateshead
Printed and bound in the UK by Creative Print and Design Wales, Ebbw Vale
Cover design by Danny Gillespie

For a full list of publications please contact:

Earthscan Publications Ltd
120 Pentonville Road, London, N1 9JN, UK
Tel: +44 (0)20 7278 0433
Fax: +44 (0)20 7278 1142
Email: earthinfo@earthscan.co.uk
Web: **www.earthscan.co.uk**

22883 Quicksilver Drive, Sterling, VA 20166-2012, USA

A catalogue record for this book is available from the British Library

Library of Congress Cataloging-in-Publication Data

Brown, Katrina, 1960-
    Making waves : integrating coastal conservation and development / Katrina Brown,
    Emma L. Tompkins, W. Neil Adger.
        p. cm.
    Includes bibliographical references and index.
    ISBN 1-85383-912-4 (pbk.) – ISBN 1-85383-915-9 (hard)
    1. Coastal zone management. 2. Sustainable development. I. Tompkins, Emma L.,
    1966- II. Adger, W. Neil. III Title.

HT391 .B767 2002
333.91'7–dc21
                                                                    2002002877

Earthscan is an editorially independent subsidiary of Kogan Page Ltd and publishes in
association with WWF-UK and the International Institute for Environment and
Development

This book is printed on elemental chlorine-free paper

Contents

List of Illustrations

FIGURES

TABLES

BOXES

Acronyms and Abbreviations

AONB	area of outstanding natural beauty (UK)
BRMP	Buccoo Reef Marine Park (Tobago)
CANARI	Caribbean Natural Resources Institute
CARICOM	Caribbean Community
CARICOMP	Caribbean Coastal and Marine Productivity Programme
CBO	community-based organization
CGIAR	Consultative Group on International Agricultural Research
CITES	Convention on International Trade in Endangered Species of Wild Fauna and Flora
CO_2	carbon dioxide
CORDIO	Coral Reef Degradation in the Indian Ocean
CSERGE	Centre for Social and Economic Research on the Global Environment
DEFRA	Department of Environment, Food and Rural Affairs (UK)
DFID	Department for International Development (UK)
DIP	deliberative inclusionary process
EEZ	exclusive economic zone (under UNCLOS)
EIA	environmental impact analysis
ENSO	El Niño southern oscillation
EU	European Union
FAO	United Nations Food and Agriculture Organization
GCRMN	Global Coral Reef Monitoring Network
GNP	gross national product
ha	hectare
ICLARM	The World Fish Centre (International Centre for Living and Aquatic Resources Management)
IIED	International Institute for Environment and Development
IUCN	World Conservation Union
MADM	multi-attribute decision model
MCA	multi-criteria analysis
MODM	multi-objective decision model
MPA	marine protected area
NAFTA	North American Free Trade Agreement
NGO	non-governmental organization
NNR	national nature reserve (UK)
NPP	net primary production
NPV	net present value
POPs	persistent organic pollutants

Ramsar	Ramsar Convention on Wetlands
SAC	Special Area of Conservation
SPREP	South Pacific Regional Environment Programme
SSSI	site of special scientific interest (UK)
SST	sea surface temperature
THA	Tobago House of Assembly
WCED	World Commission on Environment and Development
WRI	World Resources Institute
WTP	willingness to pay
WWF	World Wide Fund for Nature
UNCLOS	United Nations Convention on the Law of the Sea
UNEP	United Nations Environment Programme

Preface

More than a billion people have their own reasons to be concerned about the sustainability of the world's coastal areas. Many of these people presently live in what we define as coastal zones and are directly or indirectly dependent on the integrity of coastal ecosystems, infrastructure and the wider environment. The extent of the world's coastal zones coupled with the number of people affecting or affected by them makes the challenge of sustainability in coastal zones extremely daunting and far-reaching. We are increasingly receiving warnings of degradation and environmental instability in these areas, from depleted fish stocks to the accumulation of persistent pollutants. We believe that the way forward is to recognize the diversity of institutions, systems of knowledge and incentives that together constrain and enable decisions on conservation and development. This strategy depends on breaking out of the status quo and, we argue, requires reform in the institutions of management in particular. It requires us to 'make waves'.

Much of the focus of this book comes from collaborative research we have carried out in the Caribbean over the past decade. We also draw on insights from our research in the Pacific, South-East Asia, East Africa and Europe. The scope of the issues is potentially enormous, and the analysis is necessarily inter-disciplinary. Our book focuses on multiple-use resources, conservation and protected areas, and environmental dilemmas on the coast.

The collaboration between the three of us began in the mid-1990s with an exploration of the trade-offs among users of marine protected areas in Trinidad and Tobago, with a view to determining how these trade-offs could be evaluated. This collaboration included researchers from the St Augustine, Trinidad campus of the University of the West Indies, notably Professor Peter Bacon and Kathy Young, and individuals within the government of Trinidad and Tobago, most importantly, David Shim and Nadra Nathai Gyan. We then considered the opportunities for and constraints to participatory coastal zone management in the Caribbean, and focused on the institutional issues surrounding participatory resource management. We are extremely grateful to the individuals mentioned above, and to our many other formal and informal collaborators, both individuals and institutions, who have helped us and supported us in many different ways throughout the evolution of our research. We have learned much from many different people.

We thank the UK Department for International Development (DFID) for funding some of the underlying research and the production of this volume through their Natural Resources Systems Programme, and we would especially like to thank Dr Margaret Quin and her team at HTS Development for their support and belief in the relevance of our endeavours. This book therefore forms an output from these projects funded by DFID for the benefit of developing countries. The views expressed are not necessarily those of DFID. We are also grateful for funding and support from the Economic and Social Research Council, through the Programme on Environmental Decision-Making within the Centre for Social and Economic Research on the Global Environment (CSERGE), and to the Leverhulme Trust.

We thank colleagues in the Overseas Development Group and in CSERGE at the University of East Anglia for discussions and interactions. We have also enjoyed feedback from many other academics, policy-makers and coastal management practitioners at various meetings in which we have presented parts of this research.

Katrina Brown, Emma Tompkins and Neil Adger
July 2002, Norwich

Chapter 1

Conservation and Development

Four thousand years ago Early Bronze Age Britons built a wooden monument near the coast of East Anglia in eastern England. Some time after it was built the monument was buried under sand by the encroaching sea. Four thousand years later in the Information Age, and following a winter storm, the beach was washed away and the monument was revealed. In the intervening 4000 years, the inhabitants of East Anglia had survived invasions, migrations and technological transformations such that the Early Bronze Age Britons would not have recognized the modern coast. The modern Information Age Britons marvelled at the Early Bronze Age technology, wondered what the hewn-timber monument could mean, and named the structure Seahenge.

Seahenge is made up of an upturned whole oak tree surrounded in a circle by 55 smooth-hewn timber columns about 4m high. The timbers were fashioned using 30 to 40 different axes made of bronze that came from Cornwall. The whole structure is 50m in diameter and was an eerie sight rising from the tidal sands. No-one knows for sure why Seahenge was built. It must surely have had religious significance and was certainly a meeting place for the ancient Britons from this corner of England. Early Bronze Age Britons traded up and down the coast and with the near continent of Europe, although the structure was built long before any contact with Roman or Norse settlers or conquerors. Seahenge is a link to the past in coastal Britain.

But, it was not long after Seahenge was uncovered in 1998 that the conflicts began. Archaeologists wanted to remove the monument to laboratories to analyse the timbers. Land-owners wished to re-build the monument on dry land to attract tourists to eastern England. Druids argued that this religious icon should be left in place – eventually it would be covered by the shifting coastal sands and perhaps reappear 4000 years from now for East Anglians from another age to marvel at.

Seahenge encapsulates our modern dilemma. Coasts are dynamic and restless entities, and define the edge of human habitation. If we desire to conserve the nature of coasts, we must conserve their dynamism – but this is not always easy. Coasts are attractive places where we have congregated throughout human history. They contain much human heritage. They are contested places. Decisions about the conservation or use of coastal areas always raise conflicts of values, interests and political power. In many ways these conflicts come down to whose values count in society. The conflicts over managing coastal zones are a set of trade-offs between values and interests, articulated through science and power, and resolved and mediated through institutions.

A new form of interdisciplinary and adaptive science is required for the coast. Such a science requires both an understanding of global environmental processes and their regional and place-specific manifestations, and also fundamental advances in our ability to address self-organization, resilience and nature–society interactions. We promote such understandings of coastal systems in this book through our focus on the social construction, legitimacy and equity of coastal institutions and resource decisions.

Throughout the world, coastal areas are important in a wide variety of ways. Everywhere they are dynamic. There are commonalities among coastal areas whether they are in rich or poor countries. Coasts have common characteristics whether coastal zones constitute the entirety of a small island or represent only a small proportion of the area of a large continental country. In this book we focus on the commonalities in terms of institutions and the prospects for resolving the conservation and development dilemmas inherent in modern coastal regions through novel institutions and new ways of identifying and dealing with trade-offs. Our insights come from action research on understanding and negotiating coastal conflicts to promote more sustainable and equitable development. The sustainable development and conservation of coastal areas is vital for the well-being and health of the world's population, including the poor. It is also vital because conservation provides the opportunities for the sea to throw up its natural and human wonders, as it did with Seahenge in East Anglia in 1998.

Coastal zones are among the most highly productive, densely populated and valuable ecosystems on the Earth. The coastal margins constitute just 8 per cent of the world's surface area but provide 25 per cent of global primary productivity. The coastal zone provides homes and livelihoods for billions of people worldwide. Perhaps 70 per cent of the global human population live within one day's walk of the shore, but this also constitutes a risk: 100–250 million people live below maximum storm surge levels (Turner and others, 1996). Two-thirds of the world's great cities are on the coast – more than 65 per cent of cities with a population of more than 1.5 million are on the coast (Crooks and Turner, 1999). In addition, the human population is increasing rapidly in these areas, so that in developing countries the population at the coast is increasing at twice the rate of other regions. In some countries the majority of the population lives on the coast: for example, in Mozambique 75 per cent of the population lives on a coastal strip 40km wide, and in Bangladesh 80 per cent of people live in the Bengal delta. In some countries, effectively all the people live on the coast. Coastal zones are thus hugely important economically. Many key industries are situated at the coast or on river mouths, and 90 per cent of the world fish harvest, representing 5–10 per cent of world food production, comes from within national exclusive economic zones, most of them within sight of shore. They are also subjected to serious natural hazards, from coastal hurricanes and typhoons through to tsunamis. The global human population potentially exposed to present and future coastal hazards has been estimated as somewhere over 1.2 billion people (Nicholls and Small, 2002).

Coastal systems link land and marine ecosystems and therefore cover a wide range of biophysical characteristics. The world's coastal zones are differentiated by climate, currents and substrate and range from the flat coastal plains of Italy, the UK and the Netherlands, to the mangroves and coral reefs around islands in the Caribbean and the Pacific, to the rugged fjords of Norway and Chile. But there are many different definitions of what constitutes a coastal zone. For example, coastal zones in small islands are in effect the entire island when they are defined as the watersheds that feed immediate seas and the adjacent marine area. The diversity of definitions of coastal zones reflects a tension between ecological and physical sciences recognizing the dynamic characteristics of the coast, and legal and political classifications. In general, definitions tend to include both land and ocean components; have boundaries that are flexible and determined by the influence of the land on the ocean and vice versa; and are not of uniform width, depth or height.

Classifications tend to mix ecological characteristics with legal definitions. In reality, a coastal zone is often designated administratively and hence managed in geographically finite units, such as the land and the sea within the 200-mile zone around a shoreline. Within the coastal zone there can be a range of uses and activities, including residential, recreational, industrial, commercial, waste disposal, agricultural, fishing and conservation uses. These definitional discrepancies reflect the trade-offs and dilemmas in coastal zone management. There is diversity in definition because of the diversity of uses and actors. Whatever set of characteristics is used, it is clear that the world's coastal zones are important ecologically and socially. It is also clear that these two domains are intertwined and inextricably linked. In this book we define coastal zones in both physical and human system terms. A coastal zone is the set of landward systems whose functioning and use directly affects the marine environment and the set of marine systems that exist in proximity to land, and that tend to be the jurisdiction of one country. In ecological and physical terms this definition of a coastal zone incorporates near-shore fisheries, coastal seas, coral reefs, seagrasses, river estuaries, intertidal ecosystems, beaches and dune systems, and the terrestrial systems of estuaries, deltas and watersheds close to the coastal margin. Coastal management involves deliberate intervention in human and physical coastal systems.

In effect, all natural resource management is an experiment from which we can learn about both the unpredictable nature of change in sensitive ecosystems, and about what works and what does not work in institutions. When coastal management works well it can be because it is adaptive, in the sense that social and institutional learning occurs in an iterative and socially responsible manner. For insights into adaptive ecosystem management see the work in a variety of contexts of Berkes and Folke (1998), Gunderson and others (1995), Lee (1993) and Ruitenbeek and Cartier (2001b). In this book we emphasize the social decision-making aspects of integrated and inclusive management. In particular we focus on the sensitivity of management to the legitimacy of local knowledge, the need for institutional learning at various scales, and on what we call the political economy of knowledge and inclusive processes.

This chapter proceeds by demonstrating why coastal zones are important in both the ecological and social dimensions, and the rationale for integrated and inclusive decision-making. The sharing of knowledge and the building of trust adds legitimacy and promotes the effectiveness of resource-use decisions. We demonstrate that for coastal zones in developing countries in particular, where the livelihood imperatives of sustainability and access to resources are acute, integrating conservation and development can be promoted through timely and sensitively applied decision-making tools. These include identifying and promoting stakeholder interests and dialogue, envisioning and prioritizing environmental and social outcomes through decision analysis and facilitating appropriate institutional forms for delivering legitimate decisions.

COASTAL GOODS AND SERVICES

The importance of coastal resources to humans can be characterized as a series of goods and services they provide, which underpin the lives and livelihoods of those who inhabit and use coastal areas. Ecosystems' services in this case are the conditions and processes through which natural ecosystems sustain and fulfil human life (Daily, 1997; Turner and others, 2001). These include purification of water and detoxification and decomposition of wastes, generation and renewal of soil and soil fertility, maintenance of biodiversity, stabilization of micro-climates, mitigation of floods and storm surges and support of diverse human cultures. For coastal ecosystems such as linked coral reefs, seagrasses and fringing mangroves, the goods and services and the links between them are diverse. They are illustrated in Figure 1.1. These services also maintain the productivity of ecosystems such that they provide ecological goods including seafood and other aquatic products, many pharmaceuticals, industrial products and their precursors. The world's coastal fisheries, for example, provide a significant proportion of nutritional protein for the populations of many developing countries (Allison, 2001).

Goods and services from coastal resources have been diminished over time, with the overexploitation of some resources leading to a decline in their availability, and through the undermining of particular ecosystem functions as a result of habitat destruction and pollution. Over 50 per cent of the world's tropical mangrove forests were converted or lost during the 19th and 20th centuries (Matthews and Fung, 1987). Coral reefs are increasingly under stress from a variety of sources associated with pollution and direct use. It is often posited that this overexploitation results from a lack of understanding of the values that these ecosystems have in terms of providing goods and services. Thus, there are various efforts to provide explanations of the importance of these goods and services in both ecological and, increasingly, economic terms.

One such effort to estimate the economic benefits of ecosystem services at the global scale has found that the total annual value of the goods and services from the world's ecosystems was of the same order of magnitude as the world

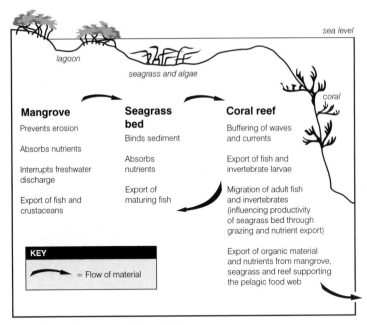

Source: Adapted from Moberg and Folke (1999)

Figure 1.1 *Ecological interactions in a coastal tropical seascape*

economy (Costanza and others, 1997). The current economic value of the non-marketed services and functions of ecosystems is US$33 trillion per year, compared to a global GNP of US$18 trillion per year. This well-known study derived the value per hectare of the world's ecosystems and biomass from published studies and scaled them up by multiplying by the area of the ecosystems to arrive at a global figure for the ecosystems' functional values.

Costanza and his colleagues argue that the non-marketed services of coastal ecosystems have higher values than all terrestrial ecosystems, some by many orders of magnitude. To examine how these estimates of value are derived, the examples of two coastal ecosystems are presented in Figure 1.2: those of mangrove and coral reef ecosystems. Figure 1.2 demonstrates that the value of these ecosystems is in the order of US$6075 per hectare (ha) for coral reefs, and US$9990 per ha for mangroves, based on the data published in Costanza and others (1997). In both cases, the major ecosystem functions that are valued are coastal protection, nutrient cycling, food production and recreation. For coral reefs, almost half their value is derived from recreational use, based on the mean of estimates of a range of economic indicators from direct revenues spent by tourists visiting coral reefs in Florida, to estimates of the economic value of recreational use in Australia, to tourist expenditures in Tahiti and Bonaire. This bias towards well-studied and accessible ecosystems and well-studied functions clearly creates distortions in the figures, which need to be treated with care.

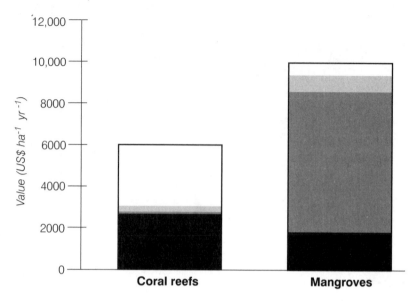

Source: Based on Costanza and others (1997)

Figure 1.2 *Composition of value elements for selected ecosystems*

For mangroves, the coastal protection function value shown in Figure 1.2 is based on the substitution cost for other protection; that for nutrient cycling is based on the replacement cost for waste-treatment plant; that for food production is based on market prices from fishing studies; and that for the recreational value of mangroves is based on estimates from Trinidad and Tobago and Puerto Rico. The Trinidad and Tobago estimate is based on a travel-cost estimate of the recreational use of Caroni Swamp in eastern Trinidad. This example of how to derive ecosystem values usefully illustrates some of the constraints on the economic dimensions of goods and services and on the extrapolation of such values.

The economic benefits of Caroni Swamp were estimated to be TT$2020 (US$200) per ha across the 5000ha of the reserve, based on estimated recreational value and fishing resources in 1974 by Rambial (1980). The non-marketed benefits estimated are recreational user benefits elicited through a survey of visitors and residents. However, this value accrues to Caroni Swamp because of the demand for the resource and the site characteristics. The mangrove area is of national significance as the only nesting site for the national emblem of Trinidad, the scarlet ibis. Large numbers of residents and foreign tourists visit Caroni Swamp because of the scarlet ibis and its unique national symbolic significance. It is also close to and easily accessible from Port of Spain, the major port of call for cruise-ship visitors and the capital city, constituting a large urban conurbation. The same demand characteristics do not apply for all mangrove forests in all locations, so the extrapolation of this value across the world's mangroves is not possible.

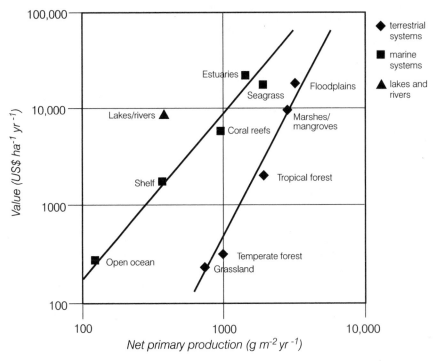

Source: Adapted from Costanza and others (1998)

Figure 1.3 *Ecological and economic values of coastal and terrestrial ecosystems compared*

Economic values of ecosystem goods and services emphasize only one particular metric and fail to capture some of the ecological complexity of coastal ecosystems. Coastal marine ecosystems are distinguished from all other ecosystems by the variability of the physical forces that influence them – they exhibit widely varying and unpredictable conditions in temperature, salinity and water movements over short timescales (Costanza and others, 1995). Estuaries are among the most vigorous of these areas and are characterized by high functional diversity, often making them ecologically resilient to perturbations. Coral reefs are, by contrast, highly diverse in species but sit within relatively narrow niches of temperature, salinity and other physical conditions.

Ecosystem goods and services are related in complex ways to the productivity, diversity and scarcity of the underlying ecosystems. The availability of goods for direct consumption from coastal ecosystems such as fisheries is likely to be correlated with the overall net primary production (NPP) of the ecosystem. Other services, such as climate control and aesthetic intrinsic values, are not so likely to be correlated with the productivity of the ecosystem. Figure 1.3 takes the economic values of ecosystems (from Costanza and others, 1997) and plots these against NPP (following Costanza and others, 1998). It shows that in terrestrial and marine ecosystems there are good correlations between value and productivity, with lakes and rivers as an outlying case. These data reflect that most of the economic value of coastal zones comes from the goods produced by ecosystems. There is no equivalent meaningful measure of diversity of ecosystems at this broad scale, but it could be speculated that greater ecosystem diversity is likely to be correlated with increasing value. The more indirect the services provided, however, the less they are connected directly to productivity or energy captured by the ecosystem and its availability.

Clearly any single estimate of ecosystem value or importance is open to criticism. The economic values discussed above demonstrate that there are serious constraints on determining relative economic values, and particularly on scaling these values in a manner that makes them meaningful. Similarly, ecological measures of the importance of ecosystems, such as their net productivity, tell only part of the story. But both ecology and economics demonstrate that ecosystem goods and services are undervalued in many management decisions, resulting in unsustainable use.

This leads to the next issue of why these values are ignored. Economists frequently argue that improvements in understanding the economic value of coastal functions will result in more sustainable use. Similarly, coastal scientists also identify lack of information as a constraint on desirable use (Barbier, 1993; Kusler and others, 1994). To characterize this argument: more information and better decision-making are required because unsustainable use is undertaken on the basis of incomplete information. Thus, it is argued, the demonstration of the services provided by ecosystems and of the economic value of the functions discussed above will increase the chances of sustainable utilization. But any values accrue to individuals who have vested interests in ignoring the implications of their decisions. Thus, we argue in this book that decision-making structures, property relations and the institutions that give them authority, underpin and determine the values, the motivations and the market structure under which sustainable utilization of natural resources in coastal zones can take place. Particular stakeholders have, in other words, good reasons to underplay or ignore ecosystem values. The long-term sustainability of ecosystems is only one element in the real politics of coastal management.

OBSERVED CHANGES IN COASTAL ZONES

Coastal zones have societal importance and value, but are these systems being degraded by overuse and human interventions? It appears that there is growing evidence of observed deleterious change. For example, Jackson and others (2001) describe a global 'collapse' of coastal ecosystems, primarily brought about by human action. But their analysis shows that although rates of change and the magnitude of human impacts on ecosystems are accelerating they are not just a recent phenomenon. Human activities have modified coastal systems for millennia in what Jackson and others call the aboriginal, colonial and global eras. The current global era is causing changes that have the most profound and negative impacts on coastal systems. Jackson and others argue that human expansion and the activities that drive change follow a sequence, but that fishing, and more specifically overfishing, is a prime factor in the deterioration of coastal ecosystems worldwide. The drivers and impacts of change are often inter-connected and, in many cases, negatively synergistic and unpredictable.

This evidence of environmental decline points to the need for learning from past mistakes and promoting adaptive management. No significant areas of the world's coastal zones, with the possible exception of parts of Antarctica, are immune from direct human impacts. But the whole world, including the coast and Antarctica, is increasingly subject to systematic environmental change through, for example, global climate change. Nowhere is immune. Climate change is likely to cause stress to coastal ecosystems through changing sea temperatures and sea level rise and, added to other drivers of environmental change, chronic stress would seem to be the most common condition. Table 1.1 presents some examples from a long and depressing list of instances of environmental decline in a variety of coastal ecosystems at various scales. Direct exploitation of marine fauna and flora, in common with terrestrial environments, has led to dramatic declines in particular species. It has led to local extinctions as in the case of the Monk seal, no longer present in the Caribbean Sea where it was abundant 300 years ago. But pollution loading of coastal waters also contributes to coastal eutrophication and water quality decline. For many of the examples in Table 1.1, isolating the individual cause of environmental decline is difficult: the immediate causes are a combination of land use change, overexploitation, and nutrient and pollution loading into coastal waters (for example, Rawlins and others, 1998).

Fisheries

One of the most significant areas of change has occurred in fisheries. The global marine fish harvest has increased six-fold since 1950. But the rate of increase annually for fish caught in the wild has, according to data from the World Resources Institute (WRI), slowed from 6 per cent in the 1950s and 1960s to 0.6 per cent in the mid-1990s (WRI, 2001). The catch of low-value species has risen as the harvest from higher-value species has reached a plateau or declined, masking some effects of overfishing. According to the United Nations Food and Agriculture Organization (FAO), one-quarter of the world's fish stocks are currently overfished, depleted or recovering from collapse and one-half are fully exploited. Such figures have led many to identify a global crisis in fisheries (Allison, 2001) and to place this as a major contribution to coastal ecosystem collapse. This crisis has serious ramifications for some of the poorest communities in the world, as predicted by Jackson and others. Of the 120 million people involved in activities related directly to the capture, processing and sale of fish, perhaps 95 per cent live in developing countries (FAO, 2000). Furthermore, although fish supply approximately 6 per cent of the world's protein requirements, they are particularly important as a source of micro-nutrients, minerals and essential fatty acids to people in low-income food deficit countries (Allison, 2001).

Fisheries in coastal areas and in small-island developing states in the tropics are made up of both artisanal and small-scale commercial fisheries. The inshore fisheries are often dependent on the coastal ecosystems of coral reefs and

Table 1.1 *Examples of historical coastal ecosystem changes caused by overfishing and pollution*

Environmental parameter	Location	Baseline and period of observation (years before present time)	Trend	Proxy measured	Cause
Coral	Caribbean Sea	125,000–present	5.3-fold decline	% sites with *A. palmata* dominant	Overfishing
Coral	Bahamas	125,000–present	12-fold decline	Abundance of *A. cervicornis*	Overfishing
Coral	Netherlands Antilles	27–present	1.7-fold decline	Coral cover at 10m	Overfishing
Monk seal	Caribbean Sea	300–present	Extinction	Sightings and documents	Overfishing
Seagrass beds	Tampa Bay	121–present	3-fold decline	Area	Overfishing and mechanical habitat destruction by fishing and pollution
Dugong	Eastern Australia	100–present	74-fold decline	Herd size	Overfishing
Eutrophication	Chesapeake Bay	1900–present	5-fold increase	Total organic carbon	Mechanical habitat destruction by fishing and pollution
Eutrophication	Gulf of Mexico	100–present	3.3-fold increase	Total organic carbon	Pollution
Eutrophication	Adriatic Sea	170–present	6-fold increase	Eutrophic benthic *Foraminifera*	Pollution
Oyster reefs	Foveaux, New Zealand	34–present	8-fold decline	Oyster landings	Mechanical habitat destruction by fishing

Source: Jackson and others (2001)

seagrasses. The largely negative impacts of cumulated environmental change from pollution and habitat change, as well as the potential of combined rises in sea levels and surface temperatures in the future, represents a very serious threat to near-shore fisheries in tropical coastal areas. For many deep-sea fisheries the interaction between the El Niño southern oscillation (ENSO) and fisheries production is a crucial issue, particularly if the increased frequency of El Niño events is linked to future climate change. There is increasing evidence that anomalous ENSO-type events are linked to 'red tide' events, where fish stocks become unavailable for human consumption. This is the case in the Atlantic, for example, where the fisheries of the Beguela current support the fishers of Namibia and a host of other coastal countries in Africa (Boyer and others, 2000).

An increase in the frequency of harmful algal blooms and hypoxia has been observed over recent decades. This may indicate that some coastal ecosystems have exceeded their ability to absorb nutrient pollutants. Some industrial countries have improved water quality by reducing inputs of certain persistent organic pollutants (POPs), but chemical pollutant discharges are increasing on a global scale with the intensification of agriculture and the use of new synthetic compounds. Although large-scale marine oil spills are declining, oil discharges from land-based sources and regular shipping operations are increasing. Traces of oil-based chemical pollutants appear in coastal seas and in the open ocean many thousands of miles from human habitation. Commercial species such as Atlantic cod, five species of tuna, and haddock are threatened globally, along with several species of whales, seals and sea turtles. Invasive species are frequently reported in enclosed seas, such as the Black Sea, where the introduction of Atlantic comb jellyfish caused the collapse of fisheries.

Tourism

Tourism is the fastest-growing sector of the global economy, accounting for US$3.5 trillion in 1999. Coastal areas worldwide are major destinations for international and domestic tourism. Some areas have been degraded by this rise in tourism in terms of both ecosystems and the human environment. The feedback effect of coastal degradation on the tourism industry itself is unknown. Tourism is often the mainstay and major economic driver of the economies of small coastal countries and small islands. Tourism is often as much dependent on a clean and pristine environment as on the services and facilities provided by coastal hotels, airports and road transport. Yet tourism has immense social and cultural impacts on coastal areas that previously have been relatively insulated from the world economy, or that have been overwhelmed by booms in tourist numbers (Brown and others, 1997).

Expansion of tourism in a particular locality often follows a cyclical pattern as depicted in Figure 1.4, which is derived from the work of Butler (1980) and others. As a destination becomes more popular with domestic or international tourists, investment in infrastructure follows and the capacity for handling ever larger numbers of visitors is consolidated. But once a plateau is reached, it is often difficult to maintain demand for the social and environmental reasons outlined. The social and cultural impacts of tourism can result in a rapid evolution of attitudes to visitors from receptive euphoria to overt hostility. Such changes in attitudes are often precipitated by the decline in local economic benefit from tourism as large externally owned and operated hotels and infrastructure move in. But in coastal areas reliant on pristine environments to attract visitors in the first place, the negative impact of increasing visitors on water quality in particular can be catastrophic. Thus, when the social and environmental carrying capacity of an individual area is breached, it can move into a period of stagnation or decline. In the Maldives, the solution appears to

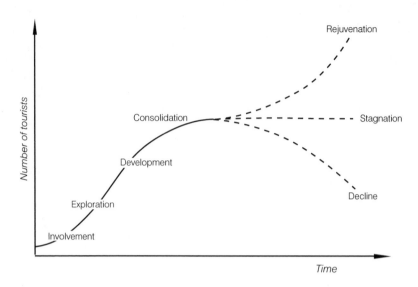

Source: Adapted from Butler (1980)

Figure 1.4 *The tourism life cycle for a coastal destination*

be to open up new destinations at the 'frontier' of uninhabited atolls (Brown and others, 1997), leaving degraded atolls to decline in popularity. Such frontier tourism is clearly unsustainable in the long run.

The extent of the pressure of numbers on small islands where coastal tourism predominates is shown in Figure 1.5. This shows a cluster of small island states economically dominated by the tourism industry and overwhelmed by visitors. Tourist arrivals in 1997 constituted five times the resident population for the Bahamas and over 100 per cent the resident population for many other small island states. For countries such as the Maldives, tourism constitutes 95 per cent of the economy and is virtually the only export activity (see Table 1.2). For these countries the pressures brought by tourism on infrastructure, particularly on water availability, sewage and solid waste management, are the most important environmental challenges. De Alberquerque and McElroy (1992) cite mounting evidence of beach erosion, reef destruction, inshore pollution and declines in scenic amenities across numerous small tourist-dependent islands in the Caribbean, which apparently confirms an incompatibility of mass tourism strategies with sustainable development (see also Pattullo, 1996). Although the concept of a tourist carrying capacity has been suggested as a tool to define an upper limit to tourist numbers, there is no hard and fast rule for any cultural context. Rather, it is the quality of the experience and the impact of each tourist that is more important. Certainly, alternative models to mass tourism should be promoted (Collins, 1999). Identifying and promoting sustainable tourism strategies exemplify the kinds of trade-offs between conservation and development that challenge sustainable coastal resource management in many countries.

Table 1.2 *Tourist arrivals and their economic importance for selected small island states*

	Tourists as % population	Tourism as % GNP	No of tourists (000)
Bahamas	586.4	42.0	1618
Antigua and Barbuda	364.2	63.4	232
Malta	294.7	22.9	1111
Cyprus	280.7	24.0	2088
St Kitts and Nevis	210.5	30.6	88
Singapore	209.2	6.2	7198
Barbados	182.4	39.2	472
Seychelles	166.7	34.6	130
St Lucia	164.7	41.1	248
Maldives	130.7	95.0	366
Grenada	116.2	27.0	111
Dominica	97.6	15.9	65
St Vincent	54.6	23.8	65
Mauritius	46.4	15.7	536
Jamaica	45.6	31.6	1192
Fiji	45.3	19.2	359
Samoa	31.1	19.6	68
Trinidad and Tobago	28.7	4.2	324
Dominican Republic	28.1	13.6	2211
Vanuatu	27.1	19.3	49
Cape Verde	11.4	11.5	45
Cuba	10.5	8.8	1153
Comoros	4.9	10.6	26
Solomon Islands	3.7	2.8	16
Haiti	2.2	3.9	149
Papua New Guinea	1.5	2.1	66

Source: Data from World Tourism Organization

Small islands and coral reefs

As we have already illustrated, coastal resources are of special importance to small islands and small island developing states. In effect, many small islands consist entirely of a coastal zone. Thus small islands are particularly dependent on coastal resources and on maintaining the ecological health and integrity of the coastal zone. They may be physically vulnerable, for example, to storm damage or climate change-induced sea level rise, but they are also economically and socially vulnerable through demographic changes, migration or the impacts of economic globalization. It has long been recognized that small island states, particularly those that are developing nations, have a unique set of circumstances making them vulnerable to external shocks from political, economic or environmental sources, and making sustainable development difficult to achieve (Streeten, 1993; Briguglio, 1995).

Coral reefs and their management are a particular focus in this book as they are among the most species-rich ecosystems on Earth. They are some of the most structurally complex and taxonomically diverse marine ecosystems,

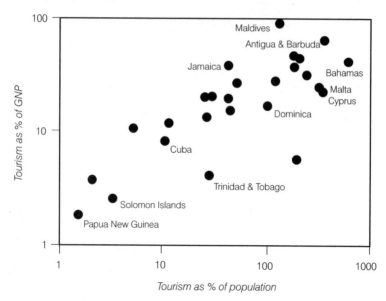

Figure 1.5 *How many is too many? Dependence of small economies on tourism*

providing habitat for many tens of thousands of fish and associated invertebrates. For this reason a large proportion of conservation interest is focused on coral reefs. But coral reefs are also highly productive systems, producing many useful species and raw materials, and providing ecosystem services such as protecting coastlines from storm damage. There is a marked and alarmingly accelerated deterioration in the status of coral reefs at a global scale (Dubinsky and Stambler, 1996; Wilkinson, 2000).

Coral reefs are important components of coastal ecosystems, providing a range of valuable economic, social and environmental services at the local, national, regional and even international levels for small island developing states. The Turks and Caicos Islands, for example, are a significant exporter of lobster and conch – this fishery is dependent on the health of coral reef systems. In the Turks and Caicos Islands, five fish processing plants processed US$1 million of conch and US$2 million of lobster in 1998 for export. By contrast, other fish, such as finfish, are important for local consumption in the Turks and Caicos Islands. The importance of coral reefs in sustaining fisheries and other services is increasingly recognized and the value of the resources within coral reef ecosystems to livelihoods is becoming more widely understood. Diverse economic goods from reef systems include seafood products, raw materials for medicines and fish. Reefs also provide socially beneficial ecological services, in that they support recreation, provide aesthetic value and support livelihoods of communities, as well as numerous other services.

In addition, coral reefs provide a range of ecological services. These services can be grouped into physical structure services, biotic services, biogeochemical services and informational services. Physically, coral reefs provide shoreline protection, promote growth of mangroves and seagrasses and generate coral sand. The biotic services provided include the maintenance of habitats, the maintenance of biodiversity and a genetic library, regulation of ecosystem processes and functions, and maintenance of biological resilience (Souter and Linden, 2000; Moberg and Folke, 1999).

Periodic natural disturbance is increasingly believed to be an important element promoting the diversity and resilience of coral reef ecosystems (Nyström and others, 2000). But coral reef resilience is reduced through chronic stress as a result of human activities on land, for example, through agricultural pollution or poorly treated sewage. Resilience can also be reduced through inappropriate fisheries management, indirect mechanisms such as land development or clearance, or natural impacts. Natural impacts come from hurricane damage (Lugo and others, 2000) and freshwater inputs from floods or heavy rains. In the Caribbean, dust blown across the Atlantic from Africa can smother coral reefs or bring disease (Shinn and others, 2000). However, the cycle of disturbance and renewal through these natural perturbations can be disrupted by chronic human impacts. Evidence is growing that global climate change is affecting coral reefs through various mechanisms.

Freshwater runoff lowers salinity and deposits large amounts of sediments and nutrients. Global surveys of the world's coral reefs, such as ReefBase, show that 56 per cent of reefs are classified as threatened. Ten per cent of the world's reefs are severely damaged or destroyed. These typically have been mined for sand and rock, reclaimed for development, or buried under sediment. Table 1.1 presents examples of decline in coral reef status as a result of overfishing, but other human actions are equally degrading. For the British Virgin Islands, for example, a survey of coral reefs reported by Wilkinson (2000) shows that the main threats to the reef systems in these islands come from sewage associated with population growth, shoreline development and sedimentation, and a rapid growth in recreational activities such as yachting, diving and snorkelling.

Climate change

Climate change threatens coastal systems around the world. Human-induced global warming could have five main impacts on coral reefs: sea surface temperature increases, sea level rise, reduced calcification rates, altered ocean circulation patterns and increased intensity or frequency of severe weather events (Done, 1999; Westmacott and others, 2000). Coral reefs usually occur and thrive within a narrow range of parameters of salinity, temperature, and nutrient and sediment loads. Climatic changes are expected to alter the environment in which corals currently grow, and very possibly change the composition of coral reefs of the future. Of the five direct potential impacts of climate change, the most serious threats are the impact of rising sea surface temperatures and higher concentrations of atmospheric carbon dioxide (CO_2) (Hoegh-Guldberg, 1999).

The impact of changes in sea surface temperature has already been felt and the consequent mass coral reef mortality that resulted through coral bleaching has been experienced around the world (Reaser and others, 2000; Brown and others, 2000). Coral bleaching, which arises from the loss of the symbiotic algae, usually results in coral death. However, debate continues in the scientific community as to the size of the contribution of anthropogenically induced global climate change to coral bleaching events. Recent evidence suggests that tropical sea surface temperatures (SSTs) have been rising over a 50-year period, and in 1998 SSTs reached the highest on record during the major El Niño–La Niña change in climate (Reaser and others, 2000). In the same year, coral reefs around the world suffered the most severe bleaching on record. Large-scale bleaching episodes, such as the 1998 El Niño event, are usually attributable to high SSTs and low light conditions. By contrast, small-scale, localized bleaching is more likely to result from direct anthropogenic impacts, such as high turbidity and sedimentation from pollution.

Coral reefs, which provide the important service of shoreline protection, are not expected to be able to grow at the rate at which the sea level is predicted to rise (Westmacott and others, 2000). Reef growth is likely to be constrained by additional stresses such as increased land-based sources of pollution, rising SSTs and increased atmospheric concentration of CO_2. If corals are unable to grow and build at their 'normal' rates they will no longer act as a breakwater for low-lying areas. The loss of protection to mangroves, seagrasses and coastal communities could cause coastal erosion and the loss of ecological habitats.

There are diverse pressures on the integrity of the world's coastal resources. The examples of threats to the ecological integrity of coral reefs are mirrored in many other coastal ecosystems. Coral reefs, along with estuaries, beaches and other physical coastal forms, are characterized by complexity and dynamism. Ecological boundaries are often less well defined in the ocean than on land and tend to be less static. For example, the boundary between fresh water flowing out of a river and salt water in the receiving ocean changes shape and location depending on the amount and speed of the freshwater flow, which can change on a daily, seasonal and annual basis. Linkages between marine systems are often complex and occur on a large scale, with nutrients and larvae as well as pollution being carried over large distances on ocean currents. Cetaceans, large pelagic fish, turtles and other species migrate huge distances to breeding and feeding grounds. These species cross ecological as well as national and sub-national political and administrative boundaries. Furthermore, in comparison with terrestrial ecosystems very little is known about marine processes and populations.

This complexity, and these dynamics, present very critical challenges for the sustainable management of coastal resources. From an ecological perspective the linkages between different components and ecosystems within coastal systems – typically the impacts of land-based activities on marine habitats and species – challenge scientific understandings and also the institutions that manage different components.

COASTAL ZONE MANAGEMENT

Given a set of economic and ecological pressures on coastal resources it is clear that effective institutions for management are required. Finding a balance between satisfying competing present-day demands without compromising the potential for future users of coastal resources to maintain their well-being is one of the central objectives of coastal zone management.

Coastal zone management is complex in the sense that decisions are always taken in an environment of uncertainty. It is complex because the co-evolution of humans decisions and physical and biological systems are in some senses inherently unknowable. The complexity stems from the same factors that make coastal zones such important resources. Coastal zones provide a range of different goods and services to many diverse users. They are often transboundary resources spanning neighbouring nations or regions: it is difficult to restrict access to them. There are many different natural environments at the land–water interface, and each environment has the capacity to affect the others. Coastal zones play important cultural roles and support social interactions in diverse ways.

Given the diversity of the functions and users of coastal zones, management can become mired in conflict and disagreement. It is therefore necessary to engage stakeholders to promote solutions that command broad agreement and are likely to be successfully implemented. The idea of a stakeholder society emerged in the 1990s to signify a symbiosis between parts of society that are normally in conflict: managers and workers, or government and business. Recognizing stakeholder interest in political spheres and co-opting groups towards shared social goals has been at the heart of a social democratic 'third way' discourse in Western democracies (Giddens, 1998). In this book we use the term 'stakeholder' to mean any individual or defined group with an interest or influence over coastal resources. We focus on conflict between stakeholders, the ability of new institutions and collective action to meet common social and environmental goals, and the broadening of stakeholder participation in decision-making and hence in coastal zone management.

Wide participation in coastal zone management on its own is not a panacea to coastal zone management problems. In cases where there are multiple users competing over scarce resources, participation may offer support to decision-makers in developing or implementing management plans. This book describes techniques to support participation in coastal zone decision-making by diverse individuals, interest groups and institutions.

Coastal management does not take place in a vacuum. It is subject to the same trends and fashions that pervade all areas of public policy and project development. When privatization is in vogue, coastal management seeks privatization solutions. When public–private partnerships are in vogue, coastal public–private partnerships are developed. Some proposals for coastal management include allocating private ownership rights to bring the resource under private or state control. Designating ownership rights is often proposed as a means to minimize the chances of overuse and overexploitation of the

Table 1.3 *Coastal zone management strategies*

Approach	Summary and objectives
Allocation of private or state property rights	Privatizing commonly owned resources or bringing them under government control to prevent overuse.
Creation of exclusive marine protected areas or restrictive zones	Marine protected areas are reserved by law or other effective means to protect part or all of the enclosed environment. They are often part of fisheries management strategies as coastal areas can act as spawning grounds for important fish species.
Integrated coastal zone management	A continuous and dynamic process that unites government and communities, science and management, private and public interests in preparing and implementing integrated plans for the protection and development of coastal ecosystems and resources.
Cooperative coastal zone management or community-based management	A framework that guides diverse and conflicting individual interests into cooperative collective decisions that draw maximum support, and enhance stakeholders' willingness to cooperate voluntarily in the implementation.
Learning-based coastal zone management	Management initiatives are implemented as experiments that must be subjected to ongoing revision in terms of developing hypotheses for testing, use of control sites, documentation of the experiment and analysis.

Sources: Crance and Draper (1996); Olsen and others (1998); White and others (1994)

coastal resources by ensuring long-term management on behalf of society. But, as we discuss in Chapter 2, private property is only appropriate for specific situations. Appropriate regimes are more likely to include state managed and collectively managed elements. Collective and state management may be out of favour in the era of 'rolling back the state', but we seek to show that the complexity of coastal resource management and the need for stakeholder inclusion mean that local solutions are going to be diverse in nature and involve all relevant institutional forms.

Zoning and allocating user rights to specific areas, engaging stakeholders in management, and creating exclusive reserves or protected areas to promote conservation have all been applied. Some of these strategies for coastal zone management are summarized in Table 1.3. The range of approaches used attests to the fact that there is still much uncertainty on how best to manage the coastal zone and there is a lack of 'blueprint' solutions.

While a variety of management approaches exists, the debate continues about the most appropriate form of management for coastal resources. There is some consensus that participation in decision-making by multiple stakeholders can contribute to the sustainable management and use of natural resources. Participation is particularly relevant for complex multiple-use resources, where conflicts can develop over management objectives. It is also relevant where different stakeholders' needs may lead to use conflicts. In these cases participation can lead to more robust management processes, particularly for small island states, where participatory decision-making can enhance self-reliance while maintaining resource integrity.

Despite the fact that coastal areas have been managed for various purposes over thousands of years, the science of integrated coastal zone management is still in its infancy. Many strategies within coastal zone management have restricted both access to and use of the resources, as in the case of establishing 'marine protected areas'. The first recorded marine protected area was established to regulate the collection of marine organisms from the Great Barrier Reef in Australia in 1906 (Sumaila and others, 1999), although traditional resource management approaches that have been in place for many hundreds of years have often involved setting aside areas to prevent overexploitation. The establishment of marine protected areas became common practice in the 1970s. By 1994 over 1000 marine protected areas had been established globally, although many existed in name only (Ticco, 1995). Failure to achieve conservation and development goals through the implementation of marine protected areas has been largely attributed to the absence of political support, financial support, stakeholder participation in the design, development and implementation, and information and education for the decision-makers and the resource users (Sumaila and others, 1999; Alder, 1996; Ticco, 1995).

But problems with the legitimacy, implementation and design of protected areas for conservation do not mean that they should simply be shunned or discarded. When they work they can promote social cohesion and ecosystem resilience and can even enhance economic interests. One such example of apparent success is the Soufrière Marine Management Area in St Lucia in the West Indies. Here, collaborative co-management was instigated and promoted to overcome conflicts between tourist interests and local fishing. In a series of iterative developments since 1995, stakeholders got together to develop co-management strategies for the area, sharing responsibility between users and regulators. Communities and stakeholder interests are not homogenous and the road to adaptive management of marine protected areas is far from smooth (see Sandersen and Koester, 2000). In later chapters we outline lessons from the adaptive management experience of Soufrière Marine Management Area.

But what is clear is that fisheries surrounding this area on the leeward coast of St Lucia have benefited from the designation of the protected area. Figure 1.6 presents results from ecological studies by Roberts and others (2001) that show clearly that the available biomass of fish species increased significantly almost immediately after the designation of the marine management area in 1995, and that this increase was more spectacular for those zones where fishing was banned. This has been to the benefit of the local artisanal fishing industry, as well as representing a showcase marine protected area for the tourism industry.

The data in Figure 1.6 also show a dip in fish biomass in 2000 following disturbance of the reef ecosystems by Hurricane Lenny, which blew through the Windward Islands in 1999. Such periodic disturbances in the past have been shown to be important in triggering renewal and development of reef diversity.

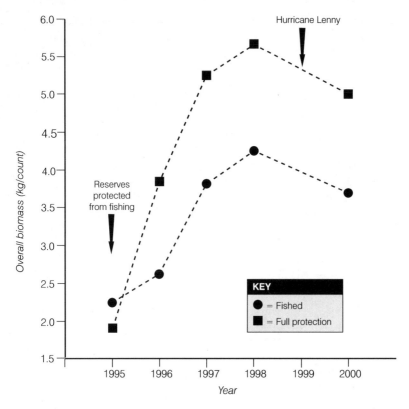

Source: Roberts and others (2001)

Figure 1.6 *Changes in commercially important fish species in adjacent fishing grounds with the implementation of Soufrière Marine Management Area, St Lucia*

The existence of the marine protected area and its successful management are of added significance if they can help reefs and fisheries recover from natural disturbances such as hurricane damage.

In order to meet the challenges of coastal zone management, an understanding of the natural and social systems in coastal zones is required. The defining characteristic of integrated approaches to coastal management is that they recognize the complexity of ecosystems, the interaction between different ecosystems, the linkages between human activity and ecosystem health, and the need for integrated interdisciplinary management. The interaction and integration between these factors have vertical and horizontal elements. Horizontal integration means joined-up decision-making concerning economic sectors such as fisheries, tourism and transport by the appropriate government agencies that influence, affect or manage coastal ecosystems. Vertical integration in this context is joined-up decision-making by all levels of government and civil society that influence, affect or manage coastal ecosystems, from local through to provincial, national, regional and international.

In other words, horizontal integration refers to the cross-sectoral harmonization of policy and practice relating to coastal zone management, and vertical integration refers to the different scales of governance, from local to international, involved in coastal zone management. Equally important are the management structures that exist and the potential for change within those structures, whether they are institutions, property rights or communities. The bringing together of the natural and social sciences within such an integrated framework, coupled with a learning-based management system, may enable gains to be made in the science of coastal zone management. As the knowledge base about the impacts of human activities on the coastal zone grows, so the management strategies used need to evolve (Olsen and others, 1997). Learning from past errors within the management process may generate a coastal zone management process that responds to the needs of the coastal zone stakeholders.

TOWARDS INCLUSION AND INTEGRATION

This book presents a set of techniques to address the dilemmas between conservation and development outlined here. These techniques focus on including the values and interests of all those concerned with coastal resources in decision-making processes. Such inclusion is often a threat to established interests and, as a result, there are many examples where only lip-service is paid to participatory, inclusive or community-based planning, specifically to limit its effectiveness. We argue that apparently conflicting interests often, in fact, have common ground that can be built on to mobilize novel and appropriate institutions for inclusive decisions.

Without understanding the institutional and political context and the dynamics and special properties of coastal systems, integrated conservation and development remains elusive. In this opening chapter we have outlined why coastal resources are important and valuable resources. We have highlighted some trends in the physical, biological and economic uses and abuses of coastal zones, particularly in terms of ecosystem decline and in the importance of coasts as the locations of tourism. Tourism is frequently the single most important economic activity for tropical coastal countries. As a phenomenon of an economically globalizing world, tourism also represents a massive environmental pressure on coastal ecosystems as well as a challenge to local cultural and social stability. We have also outlined challenges to coastal management from coral reefs as a threatened and centrally important ecosystem of tropical coastal zones. Threats arise from the global expansion of the use of coasts as well as from systemic global environmental changes such as climate change.

These phenomena and trends demonstrate a growing and urgent need for the integration of economic, social and ecological perspectives on the management of coastal resources. The techniques outlined in the following chapters promote the inclusion of stakeholders in defining scenarios and planning through decision analysis and in facilitating conflict resolution for inclusive decisions. Ultimately, the sustainable use of coastal resources is a global goal, promoted internationally, for example, through Agenda 21 and other initiatives. In this book we focus, in particular, on the problems and dilemmas of those parts of the developing world where the natural resources of the coast form significant and necessary resources for livelihood resilience. Here the dilemmas and trade-offs for sustaining the coast are acute and immediate. In some developing (and indeed developed) countries, the scope and willingness of the state to engage with diverse stakeholders or to recognize traditional resource management systems may be limited. The objectives of the book are in effect to promote dialogue and understanding of decision-making processes towards this elusive sustainability goal.

Chapter 2

Institutions in the Coastal Zone

How are coastal zones managed, and by whom? In this chapter and Chapter 3 we outline the principles of governance of coastal resources. 'Governance' in this context refers to the framework of social and economic systems and legal and political structures through which the coast is managed. Much of this discussion is concerned with institutions. By 'institutions' we mean the human-devised rules that structure human interaction. Institutions are thus made up of formal constraints (rules, laws, constitutions), informal constraints (norms of behaviour, conventions and self-imposed codes of conduct) and their enforcement characteristics (North, 1990). Institutions are 'the set of rules actually used (the working rules or rules-in-use) by a set of individuals to organize repetitive activities that produce outcomes affecting those individuals and potentially affecting others' (Ostrom, 1990). Institutions include property rights, as well as legislative frameworks, government and non-governmental organizations (NGOs), and less formal collective action. We start by examining why collective action is of fundamental importance to the sustainable management of coastal resources, and then examine governance structures and organizations that typically manage the coast. As we assert, the challenge of integrating the concerns for the social, economic and ecological dimensions of coastal development and conservation strategies frequently requires reforms in management institutions at various levels.

COASTAL MANAGEMENT AS COLLECTIVE ACTION

Integrating conservation and development often demands that existing property rights are challenged, redesigned and made harmonious with the long-term goals of sustainability. Property rights refer to specific rights to utilize, control and exchange assets. So, understanding the nature of property rights and the institutions that regulate and use them is a key step in promoting representative and sustainable management. Property rights regimes are heterogeneous (including state, common, customary, private and open access), and can be well or badly managed and are dynamic.

The nature of coastal resources

The multiple resource and multiple use characteristics of coastal resources influence the structures of tenure and management regimes. At the interface of the marine and terrestrial ecosystems, there are typically huge demands for a multitude of uses and functions, which often results in conflict between different users.

Coastal resource characteristics thus provide particular challenges. Table 2.1 shows that the property rights regimes for coastal resources depend on the subtractible nature of the resource, the ease of exclusion of users and whether the resources are stationary or fugitive. 'Subtractible' means that one person's consumption reduces the availability of the resource for consumption by others. Thus, the activities of one bird-watcher generally do not reduce the number of birds available for other watchers. Leaving aside the issue of congestion in bird-watching sites, bird-watching is effectively said to be 'non-rival in consumption', or non-subtractible. Fishing is almost always subtractible.

Table 2.1 *The nature of coastal resources and typical property rights regimes*

	Easily excluded	Exclusion costly or difficult
Stationary (terrestrial)		
Subtractible (rival in consumption)	Mangrove used for fuel, construction and other timber (often private property regimes).	Hunting for fauna or birds. Collection of medical plants, poisons, tannins, fertilizers.
Non-subtractible (non-rival in consumption)	Recreational use of coastal wetlands for tourism, bird-watching.	Ecological functions such as carbon cycling in terrestrial biomass. Coastal protection function of mangroves and salt marshes. Maintenance of habitats and refugia. Maintenance of micro-climates.
Fugitive (aquatic/marine)		
Subtractible (rival in consumption)	Fishing and aquaculture production in enclosed and seasonal wetlands. Agricultural production in seasonal wetlands.	Fishing and aquatic product collection in open wetlands such as coastal areas.
Non-subtractible (non-rival in consumption)	Recreational or other non-consumptive use of coastal wetlands. Angling (often organized as club goods).	Marine and aquatic ecosystem services: regulation of food web dynamics, nutrient fluxes from water to atmosphere, sediment processes, marine biodiversity and habitats, groundwater recharge.

Source: Adapted from Adger and Luttrell (2000)

Table 2.1 follows a general typology of goods by McKean (1996) adapted for wetland resources following analysis by Buck (1989), Rönnbäck (1999), Holmlund and Hammer (1999) and others. Each coastal component tends to have different property rights regimes associated with it. These rights are attenuated by various legal and customary restrictions that define limitations on the use or consumption of the good or resource. There are several types of property rights emerging as a result of the intrinsic nature of the resource, as well as by cultural and social determinants. These range from open access to common property, state property and private property. The coexistence of contrasting communal and individual rights to resources, even within the same community, is a common feature of coastal systems. As non-fixed or 'fugitive' resources (such as fish, crabs and lobsters) move in and out of geographical boundaries, the definition of private property can become problematic. For example, since fish are fugitive resources, extractive practices or activities that affect fish stocks in one area will affect fish supplies in other areas.

Common property regimes are ruled through a group of individuals or organizations that enforce control over access and use (Baland and Platteau, 1996). In these cases, individual users of a resource tend to have greater incentives to cooperate with each other than to pursue individualist strategies, and the resource usually has well-defined boundaries. The incentives for cooperation are often associated with aspects such as economies of scale compared with individual management. Examples from fisheries management include shared gear and processing facilities and shared fishing areas. Thus, as outlined above, common property can be contrasted with privately owned or state owned property at one end of the spectrum, and open access resources where no property rights exist, as with the atmosphere and open oceans.

Commonly managed systems have been documented for marine and terrestrial resources in all regions of the world (see, for example, Ostrom, 1990; Berkes, 1989; Walters, 1994; Berkes and others, 2001; Pinkerton and Weinstein, 1995; Baland and Platteau, 1996). Oceanic fishing resources and offshore oil resources, despite their apparent open access nature, also tend to be 'governed', with varying degrees of success, through customary law or through bilateral or multilateral agreements between governments, such as the United Nations Convention on the Law of the Sea (UNCLOS) (Birnie and Boyle, 1992).

It has been proposed that those resources with open access or common property regimes require collective action to ensure sustainability as tensions can arise among resource users. A range of factors can contribute to increased tension, from changes in technology and externally imposed changes in institutional rules to changes in aspirations and values over time. Box 2.1 outlines some of these causes of tension from experience of community-based management in the Pacific by Warner (2000). In addition, the self-promoting actions of individuals in coastal areas invariably lead to overexploitation of open access public goods. This is not to say that individuals only act selfishly: cultural and social institutions ensure that this is not the case. The tension between social and individual objectives reinforces the need for appropriate institutions of collective action to mediate the economic forces and trends of global change described in Chapter 1.

Box 2.1 Factors contributing to tension over common property resource management and use

1 *Productivity-enhancing technologies.* If poorly managed, new technology such as new fertilizers, agricultural mechanization, permanent irrigation and so on can lead to overuse of renewable resources.
2 *Awareness of resource value.* Growing stakeholder awareness of the commercial value of their resource, wildlife, land, minerals, forests, fish and so on can lead to excessive extraction, or a push for privatization of the resource.
3 *Rising local aspirations for consumer products.* Increasing importance of a cash economy.
4 *No incentive to internalize externalities.* Social and environmental externalities that can be generated from resource use may affect third-party groups, but there may be no incentive for the resource users to manage this.
5 *Top–down conservation policies.* Introduction of any resource management initiative that excludes stakeholders.
6 *Declining economic and social support for local resource users.* Reduced government spending on rural health-support services.
7 *Rural-to-urban migration.* Creates shortages of local labour for sustainable management of common property resources.
8 *Creation of new forms of rural employment.* New industries such as fish processing, extractive industries and construction may reduce the labour available for local resource management.

Source: Warner (2000)

Institutions for Coastal Zone Management

Formal institutions for coastal management

Management of coastal resources has historically focused on managing the individual goods and services provided by the coastal zone, and ensuring the maintenance of a long-term supply of those goods and services to economic markets. This is frequently achieved through formal institutional arrangements. Formal institutional arrangements can be grouped into two areas.

- *Constitutional rules and regulations*, such as the Law of the Sea, or the regulations associated with fishing gear, fish quotas or dredging permits.
- *Organizational structures*, such as the agencies that implement or enforce the regulations, including the agents who establish legal ownership rights for excludable resources.

This section briefly outlines some of the key formal institutions responsible for coastal zone management, including legal frameworks and international regulation, state and government agencies and conservation designations.

BOX 2.2 MAJOR INTERNATIONAL MARINE ENVIRONMENTAL LAWS 1980–1995

1980	Convention on the Conservation of Antarctic Marine Living Resources (CCAMLR)
1982	UN Convention on the Law of the Sea (UNCLOS)
1987	Convention on the International Trade in Endangered Species (CITES)
1989	Salvage Treaty
1990	Hague Declaration on the Protection of the North Sea
1991	International Convention of Oil Pollution Preparedness Response and Cooperation
1991	UN General Assembly High Seas Drift Net Resolution
1992	UN Convention on Biological Diversity
1992	UN Agenda 21
1992	Convention on the Protection of the North Sea
1992 Area	Convention on the Protection of the Marine Environment of the Baltic Sea
1995	UN Agreement on Straddling and Highly Migratory Fish Stocks
1995	Global Programme of Action for the Protection of the Marine Environment from Land-based Activities
1995	Jakarta Mandate on Marine and Coastal Biological Diversity (marine protected areas)
1995	FAO Code of Conduct for Responsible Fisheries

Source: Adapted from Boersma and Parrish (1999)

Legal frameworks

More than 28 major international marine environmental laws have been established since 1946. Box 2.2 shows those that have been developed since 1980. The international treaties, conventions and regulations are varied in form and purpose. Some represent legally binding 'hard laws' with enforcement provisions, while others are more statements of intent or 'soft laws', which depend on the development of national legislation to regulate and implement their objectives, as is the case with international conventions. In addition, there is a series of multinational agreements to regulate the use of particular species and to control particular uses of marine resources.

A key international framework is UNCLOS, dating from 1982, which defines areas of jurisdiction and legal boundaries for marine and coastal areas. Under this framework convention, countries maintain sovereign rights to explore, exploit, conserve and manage living and non-living resources within their exclusive economic zone (EEZ) up to 200 nautical miles from the coastline, as shown in Figure 2.1. Other countries maintain navigation and limited transport freedoms within the EEZ, and their access to fisheries may be limited. Most coastal resources therefore lie within the boundaries of national legislation, and will depend on the legislative structures of particular countries. A number of international and regional institutions and actors therefore influence the coastal management strategies in a given country. For example,

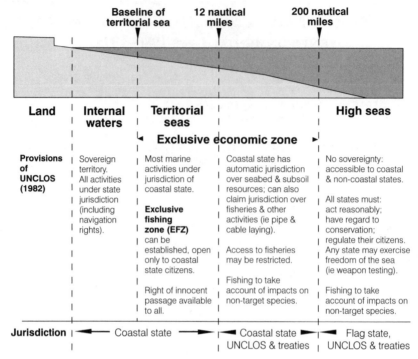

Figure 2.1 *Definitions, provisions and jurisdictions under the UN Convention on the Law of the Sea*

Source: Adapted from Allison (2001)

Box 2.3 shows the institutional actors at the supra-national level influencing coastal resource management in the Caribbean. These range from international environmental NGOs and trade groups to regional development banks.

State and government agencies
At national levels, a wide range of government and state agencies are involved in managing the coast. These agencies tend to be organized along sectoral lines and usually only address one resource issue. They tend to be grouped around:

• resource exploitation (including fisheries, forestry and mining of sand, gas, oil and other minerals);
• infrastructure development (including transport, ports, harbours, marinas, shoreline protection and national defence);
• tourism and recreation; and
• conservation and protection of biodiversity.

Thus individual institutions conventionally each take responsibility for managing separate elements of the coastal zone. The formal institutional arrangements for coastal zone management usually comprise a set of government

BOX 2.3 SUPRA-NATIONAL INSTITUTIONS IN COASTAL
MANAGEMENT IN THE CARIBBEAN

International actors

- International fisheries and marine resource management agencies including: International Maritime Organization, International Council for the Exploration of the Sea, World Commission on Protected Areas, the World Conservation Union (IUCN), UNEP's World Conservation and Monitoring Centre.
- International human development agencies including United Nations Development Programme, the World Bank.
- International NGOs including: Wetlands International, Greenpeace International, World Wide Fund for Nature (WWF).
- International research centres including: Consultative Group on International Agricultural Research (CGIAR), Global Coral Reef Monitoring Network (GCRMN), The World Fish Centre (ICLARM).
- International trade groups (eg, World Tourism Council).
- Tourists.
- Multinational corporations.

Regional actors

- Regional research organizations including the Caribbean Coastal and Marine Productivity Programme (CARICOMP).
- Regional trade groups including: European Union (EU), North American Free Trade Agreement (NAFTA), Caribbean Community (CARICOM), Caribbean Tourism Organization.
- Regional funding bodies including: Inter-American Development Bank, Caribbean Development Bank.

departments, which may include: marine resources, fisheries, forestry, agriculture, land use planning, mineral resources, trade and industry, public works and infrastructure, national defence or coastguard, customs and excise, transport, ports authority, tourism, health and environment.

Few if any of these departments are responsible for managing the entire coastal area. Each tends to specialize in only one aspect of management. For example, fisheries managers will focus on identifying stock sizes and the maximum sustainable yield of a fishery. Structural and coastal engineers assess the stability and vulnerability of coastal defences and address these through engineering projects to modify or stabilize the shoreline. Coastal water quality is usually monitored by health agencies that develop safe bathing water quality standards, such as the EU's 'Blue Flag' (Georgiou and others, 2000).

The conventional sectoral approaches of these agencies often rely on the assumption that science can always inform the management of resources better than lay knowledge, and that scientifically trained specialists are the best guides to resource management. As a result, coastal management has traditionally been exclusive in nature and top–down in implementation. The concept of the sectoral agencies whose purpose is to understand, model and manage individual coastal resources has become the accepted standard and represents the experience of most environmental planning at the national level. A review of the lessons learned from the formal institutional management of environmental planning suggests that there is little evidence of any integration of environment and development planning, as a result of the history, philosophies and roles of the formal institutions involved (Slocombe, 1993). Traditionally, planning for economic development has been the role of government urban and regional economists. Planning for the biophysical environment, on the other hand, has been undertaken by environmentalists and ecologists who have an interest in conservation. The only common ground between the two groups is that they both rely on formal management institutions and tend to exclude informal groups and stakeholders.

When individual government agencies operate independently without considering the actions of other agencies, the inconsistencies in planning become stark realities and often result in ineffective, inconsistent or even contradictory decisions. The problem of inconsistent management objectives is further exacerbated in the case of coastal zones that cross national boundaries. In such cases there are major difficulties in coordinating and enforcing action to reduce pollution across sectoral departments and across nation states.

An example is that of coordinated action for pollution control in the Baltic Sea. The northern sub-basins of the Baltic Sea have low populations, extensive forests, wetlands, lakes and a mountain terrain. The area surrounding the southern Baltic contains 55 million people (65 per cent of the total population of the countries in the area) and there is substantial agricultural activity. The Baltic Sea itself is the largest brackish body of water in the world and is naturally very sensitive to environmental change. Population growth, urbanization, agricultural intensification and land use changes in the area surrounding the Baltic Sea in the second half of the 20th century have led to an increase in the use of fertilizers, increased nitrogen fixation by crops, increased industrial and vehicle combustion emissions and the inadequate treatment of sewage, among other changes. These changes have contributed to massive nutrient pollution due to nitrogen and phosphorous loading. Many toxic algae outbreaks have occurred and eutrophication is appearing in parts of the sea. The problem partly arises from the lack of integration among the agencies involved in management, and a lack of cohesion in management objectives (Turner and others, 1999).

Conservation designations

As with legal frameworks, numerous, often overlapping conservation designations influence the management of coastal resources. These designations may derive from international agreements or from national or local government agencies. They may take a holistic ecosystem approach or they may be concerned with one particular aspect of the coastal zone, a specific habitat or species. Table 2.2 illustrates these multiple nature conservation designations in the case of the north Norfolk coastline in eastern England, the area incorporating Seahenge. Different agencies are responsible for the designation and management of these areas. For example, English Nature is the statutory agency responsible for conservation, and the Countryside Agency is responsible for access. Local conservation NGOs, including the Norfolk Wildlife Trust, are involved in the management of these areas. The designations cover different geographical scales: virtually the whole coastline is designated as a Site of Special Scientific Interest (SSSI), a Heritage Coast, a Biosphere Reserve, a Ramsar site (ie, protected by the Ramsar Convention on Wetlands) or a Special Area of Conservation (SAC). The designations therefore overlap, as Table 2.2 shows, in terms of terrestrial and marine boundaries as well as local administrative ones. The designations affect the property rights and uses of coastal resources in a variety of ways. They may, in the case of national nature reserves (NNRs), exclude virtually all access and use, or may produce recommendations and incentives for environmentally sensitive uses, as in the case of Biosphere Reserves and areas of outstanding natural beauty (AONBs). They reflect the diversity of uses and values associated with coastal resources and highlight the complexity of management given overlapping property rights, uses and interests.

Table 2.2 *Nature conservation designations in north Norfolk*

Designation	Designating body	Designation status	Reason for designation	Jurisdiction
Site of special scientific interest (SSSI)	English Nature	National	Special flora, fauna, geological or physiographical features	Terrestrial and intertidal habitats
National nature reserve (NNR)	English Nature	National	Represent the UK's best areas of natural or semi-natural habitat	Terrestrial and intertidal habitats
Area of outstanding natural beauty (AONB)	Countryside Agency	National	Conservation and enhancement of natural beauty	Landscape
Heritage coast	Countryside Agency	National	Conserve, protect and enhance the natural beauty of coasts	Landscape
Ramsar sites	EU directive	International	Designated under international convention	Wetlands
Biosphere reserve	UNESCO Man and Biosphere programme	International	Develop scientific basis for use and conservation of the biosphere	Conservation of large landscape units
Special protected area	EU directive	International	Protection of wild birds	Wetlands
Special areas of conservation	EU directive	International	Protection of habitats and species	Terrestrial and marine habitats

Source: Myatt-Bell and others (2002)

In many parts of the world, a marine protected area (MPA) is the most significant conservation designation affecting the use of and access to coastal resources. MPA is a generic term and the World Conservation Union (IUCN) defines it as 'any area of intertidal or subtidal terrain, together with its overlying water and associated flora, fauna, historical and cultural features, which has been reserved by law or other effective means to protect part or all of the enclosed environment'.

This definition is very broad and encompasses a wide range of purposes, including fisheries management, provided they have a conservation objective. There are approximately 1300 MPAs worldwide, although they account for only 1 per cent of the world's marine area. Coverage is not evenly distributed across either biological or political regions. For example, there are 267 such areas in Australia, but only four countries in Africa have designated MPAs. In addition, it is generally agreed that many of these areas exist as 'paper parks' and are poorly enforced and implemented (WWF International, 1998). The degree of protection might range from the total exclusion of all forms of use (for example, Leigh Marine Reserve, New Zealand), to restrictions on selected users and multiple use (Great Barrier Reef Marine Park, Australia), to few restrictions (for example, national marine sanctuaries in the USA) (Boersma and Parrish, 1999). MPAs therefore cover all the six categories of protected areas designated by IUCN. WWF International (1998) identifies five different types of areas: no-fishing zones, areas for pollution prevention, off-shore protected areas within national jurisdiction, MPA beyond national jurisdiction, and transfrontier or regional MPA networks. Coastal MPAs tend to fall under national jurisdiction, and may therefore be an extension of terrestrial park legislation (as in the UK) or fisheries legislation (as in the USA), or may be the responsibility of an entirely new governing area (as in the Great Barrier Reef Marine Authority in Australia) (Boersma and Parrish, 1999). The reasons for establishing MPAs are varied and rarely is there a single motivating factor. Boersma and Parrish (1999) have reviewed the reasons for the establishment of MPAs and find that almost all aimed for some form of protection of local marine resources, and in addition, cited either conservation of biodiversity, maintenance of fisheries or promotion/control of tourism as additional reasons for designation. The two principal uses of MPAs are therefore as fisheries management tools and as national parks protecting unique habitats and resident marine communities. All MPAs are in effect related to a desire to maintain or increase ecosystem values, often expressed as economic values, environmental services, ecological values and socio-cultural values.

MPAs therefore have multiple objectives. But how effective are they? WWF International (1998) believes that many existing MPAs fall short of achieving their objectives. But there is some empirical evidence that marine reserves can, if well managed, provide benefits for biodiversity conservation and fisheries management as discussed in Chapter 1 (Roberts and others, 2001). However, Kelleher (1999) claims that fewer than 50 per cent are effectively managed. An extensive survey of the state of MPA management by Alder (1996) concludes that although substantial progress has been made in the last 25 years in establishing such areas, planning and management are constrained by a number of factors including complicated legislation and a lack of funding, expertise and information. Despite the widespread promotion of integrated and multiple-use models, most MPAs are still implemented as more conventional exclusionary protected areas with little involvement by local communities and NGOs.

The apparent failure of MPAs to meet their goals cannot be attributed solely to direct issues. Many factors affecting the coastal and marine ecosystems in MPAs may be outside the control of management itself. Boersma and Parrish (1999) conclude that MPAs may be most effective as tools for managing the direct and indirect effects of resource extraction, but they cannot adequately protect marine resources in areas subject to human-mediated pollutants (for example, near-shore systems) without additional forms of protection. Nor can area-based designations provide effective protection for highly mobile species. Marine areas can, however, provide recognition of important problem areas and educational opportunities, and can shift political attention to issues of conservation and the sustainable use of marine and coastal resources. The general impression is that MPAs have potential to be effective in meeting multiple objectives but they are rarely implemented successfully.

Informal organizations for coastal management

In addition to the formal management organizations, there are usually a variety of informal organizations involved in coastal zone management, either as users or stakeholders. Informal organizations are often loose coalitions of individuals or groups with similar interests or objectives, such as private sector organizations, NGOs, trade groups or church groups. Others include community-based organizations (CBOs), which may be created out of investment in social capital or through expansion of social networks. Specific movements based on collective action tend to arise in response to a specific issue that affects many diverse individuals. Such organizations are increasingly seen as important components of more integrated approaches to coastal management, and the following chapters examine various attempts to include a range of civil society groups in coastal management.

While informal organizations and institutions have historically been overlooked by coastal zone managers in developing resource management plans, the move towards multi-disciplinary, bottom–up or ecosystem-based management approaches creates a range of challenges for conventional management institutions. Notably, the formal institutions that exist, both in terms of constitutional rules and organizational structures, often do not have the flexibility to change and adapt. To facilitate a change in management approach, however, the institutions involved in coastal zone management will most likely need to adapt. While this is difficult to implement, it is not impossible, and there are successful examples where institutional adaptation has led to the incorporation of the community and other informed institutions. A classic example is the case of the Soufrière Marine Management Area, described in Box 2.4.

BOX 2.4 CO-MANAGEMENT OF THE SOUFRIÈRE MARINE MANAGEMENT AREA IN ST LUCIA, WEST INDIES

At Soufrière in south-west St Lucia in the Caribbean, competing users of the coastal resources, particularly the fisheries and tourism industries, were exerting pressure on the coastal and marine resources. Fish stocks were depleting and the coastal resources were declining in quality. In 1986, after exploring a range of options, the government department responsible for marine resource management opted to establish zones that prioritized either fishing or conservation. Areas were thus delineated either as fishing priority areas or as marine reserves. However, these were largely unsuccessful in terms of coral or fisheries conservation. Individuals and groups concerned with the issue were not consulted and the delineation was rejected as an arbitrary, top–down management solution. Tensions persisted among users and the regulations were largely ignored.

In 1988, the Department of Fisheries came together with the Soufrière Regional Development Foundation (a local NGO) and the Caribbean Natural Resources Institute (a local research organization) to jointly tackle the stakeholder use conflicts that had mired the implementation of zoning plans for improved coastal management in earlier years. Together, the groups surveyed and mapped the coastal area, and with the aid of resource users, identified those areas used by different user groups. While the maps were similar to those drawn up in 1986 by the Department of Fisheries, the perception that these were 'everybody's maps' lent them validity. The deliberative process facilitated discussions aimed at developing a participatory management system. By 1995, the Soufrière Regional Development Foundation took the lead in promoting the Soufrière Marine Management Area, using a zoning strategy based on maps generated through dialogue with the stakeholders.

Source: Sandersen and Koester (2000); Geoghegan and others (1999).

MISMATCHED INSTITUTIONS AND CONFLICTS IN COASTAL ZONES

Given the range of institutions and interests in the coastal zone there are likely to be conflicts of interest over resource use, or instances where one use of the resource will affect other users' ability to use the resource as they wish. When conflicts occur across boundaries or spatial scales it is sometimes difficult to identify the stakeholders involved in the conflict and the nature of the conflict. Environmental problems are often created by production or consumption that takes place outside the coastal zone, yet the problem is experienced in the coastal zone. Typically such externalities are in the form of pollution, which is created inland. For example, Lapointe and Matzie (1996) reported on the effects of stormwater nutrient discharges on eutrophication processes in Florida. They explored the impacts of groundwater run-off into coastal waters following high rainfall events. The groundwater was contaminated by septic tank effluent, and they found that a lack of management of the inland septic tanks was having a noticeable impact on coral reef health. However, those creating the pollution and those suffering the impact were different stakeholder groups. Upstream resource use and land use change due to urbanization frequently impacts on coastal resources despite apparently thoughtful planning by other institutions.

Kaneohe Bay in Hawaii, for example, has suffered the effects of natural processes in the form of freshwater flooding and sediment from land erosion for many years (Hunter and Evans, 1995). Pressures imposed by human activities from the 1940s to the 1970s, including agriculture, grazing and urbanization, led to a range of changes in the state of the coast, including increased sedimentation and soil erosion, reef dredging and the direct discharge of sewage into the bay. These changes transformed the coral gardens off the coast of Kaneohe into an area most noted for high nutrient levels and turbidity and a community structure dominated by the green bubble alga *Dictyosphaeria cavernosa*. Redirecting the two large sewage outfalls away from the bay in the late 1970s led to a rapid change in water quality and community structure over the following six years: coral cover increased as the green bubble alga decreased (Hunter and Evans, 1995).

The examples from Florida and Hawaii are both cases in which off-site local stakeholders create an impact that affects on-site resource users. Conflicts can also arise at the national or international level between different nations or international agencies. Similarly, conflicts can arise across different scales. For example, in the case of sea level rise resulting from climate change, there are very complex ecological interactions on the global scale that create impacts that are felt at the local level. These transboundary or trans-scale conflicts are difficult to manage for various reasons, mostly relating to the transboundary and global nature of the problem (Nicholls and Mimura, 1998). Evidence from around the world suggests that it is rare to find close collaboration between nations leading to the creation of jointly managed protected areas. For example, in the Bay of Chetumal in Central America, unique coastal ecosystems containing interlinked marine, wetland and terrestrial habitats form the maritime border between Mexico and Belize. The ecosystems, which run from the Rio Hondo through the Bay of Chetumal to the Boca Bacalar Chico on the Caribbean coast, contain many endangered species, including the West Indian manatee (*Trichechus manatus*). In this case, informal collaboration between the Mexican and Belizean authorities has ensured some degree of protection for the manatee and the coastal ecosystems. More formalized collaboration has not occurred, however, due to questions of national sovereignty. Each country has unilaterally declared regulations pertaining to the management of the area, although the regulations differ in content and there is no transboundary agreement to implement the regulations of the other country (Lock, 1997).

Analysis of the development of transboundary protected areas and the role of international relations has generated a set of criteria for successful management by distant stakeholders. Lock (1997) proposes that to develop successful management at the international or regional level, four issues require consideration. There needs to be long-term political will among all stakeholders, equitable funding by all stakeholders for the same time period, compatible objectives in the declaration of the areas and compatible management approaches, and a commonly accepted conservation and development vision based on agreed principles.

INTEGRATION IN COASTAL ZONE MANAGEMENT

As we have seen, the institutions governing coastal zone management tend to be segregated in terms of their sectoral specializations, their scales of influence and their responsibilities for implementation. If a more holistic and integrated approach to the management of coastal resources is to be achieved, then institutions typically need to be redesigned in order to facilitate integration. Integration therefore needs to be addressed in a number of different dimensions and in a number of different ways. First there needs to be integration of social, economic and ecological considerations in order to devise sustainable management strategies. This means that formal institutions need to be better integrated *horizontally* – ie across sectors and specialisms – and *vertically*, ie across different scales of operation (local, regional, national, international). Third, there should be integration between formal and informal institutions in coastal management.

Olsen and Christie (2000) argue that coastal management does not replace traditional sector-by-sector management, but rather provides additional dimensions to government processes in order to examine and act upon the interactions and interdependencies among human activities and the ecosystem processes that link coastal lands with the coastal oceans. They suggest a simple typology that distinguishes between different degrees of sectoral integration for coastal management, as outlined in Box 2.5. The third of these categories is integrated coastal management, which aims to develop sustainable management strategies. As Alder (1996) has pointed out, however, the constraints to integration within formal government structures are considerable. We discuss these issues in later chapters.

Various mechanisms can be employed to bring about integration. For example, catchment area management or watershed management approaches have been promoted in order to generate more horizontally-integrated policy that brings many different sectors and agencies together. In cases where integrated management has been attempted, such change has meant a move away from single agency management to multiple agency management. The key to this move has been sharing information and knowledge. Indeed, Grumbine (1994) suggests that ecosystem management extends beyond science, and encompasses more than just traditional approaches to resource management. He suggests that it requires a 'fundamental reframing of how humans may work with nature' (Grumbine, 1994, p27). Thus introduction of alternative mechanisms for managing coastal resources may lead to a move away from externally imposed top–down decisions towards more bottom–up approaches.

Integration may also be attempted at different levels of governance: in other words, at community, local, regional or national scales. In many instances, integration is relied upon at a local or community scale, when single sector line ministries or departments remain in place. Some countries are attempting integration at a range of different scales or levels of governance. In the UK the development and conservation aspects of coastal management have been the responsibility of separate institutions, but a number of important changes have

Box 2.5 Degrees of sectoral integration in coastal management

Enhanced sectoral management

Focuses on the management of a particular sector or topic but explicitly addresses impacts and interdependencies with other sectors and the ecosystems affected. Investments in coastal tourism and transportation infrastructure funded by development banks increasingly feature in this approach.

Coastal zone management

Multi-sectoral management focused upon both development and conservation issues within narrow, geographically delineated stretches of coastline and near-shore waters. Many state coastal management programmes in the USA illustrate this approach.

Integrated coastal management

Expands the cross-sectoral feature of coastal zone management to consideration of the closely coupled ecosystem processes within coastal watersheds and oceans; it explicitly defines its goals in terms of progress towards more sustainable forms of development.

Source: Adapted from Olsen and Christie (2000)

been made in recent years that support more integrated approaches to coastal management. Figure 2.2 shows the responsibility for coastal zone management in England. Shoreline management plans were introduced in 1995 with the explicit objective of providing a more comprehensive and integrated approach to managing the coast. Their main purposes include the improved understanding of coastal processes; the identification of features likely to be affected by coastal change; the pinpointing of zones for special investigation; and the facilitation of consultation among bodies with an interest in the coast. Shoreline management plans should help to assess strategies options and monitor change, inform planning authorities of where development would be undesirable, identify options for maintaining and enhancing the coastal environment, and ensure continuing arrangements for consultation among interested parties. Thus the shoreline management plans aim to provide frameworks for coordination, but have little statutory power. They potentially provide important bridges between development and conservation agencies at a local level. According to O'Riordan and Ward (1997), their significance depends on informed consent and widespread support by all interested parties.

In the past, flood defence and river regulation were the responsibility of the Ministry of Agriculture, Food and Fisheries, whereas biodiversity and conservation fell under the remit of the Department of the Environment. The Environment Agency was established as the primary executive agency to integrate these aspects. Since 2001, a new department, the Department of Environment, Food and Rural Affairs (DEFRA), has been created to bring environment and agriculture together in one large ministry. We can see,

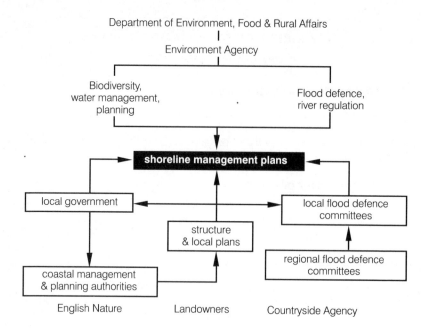

Figure 2.2 *Responsibility for coastal management in England and Wales*

therefore, that a better integration of the conservation and development aspects of coastal management has been attempted through the reorganization of these formal institutions of the state. In addition, attempts are made to include a wider range of stakeholders in consultation and planning processes, an issue discussed more fully in Chapter 3.

Integration also attempts to bring together government and civil society groups. Olsen and Christie (2000) highlight the difference between community-based management and co-management approaches. Community-based management may be characterized as a community-led process that involves the government once a community has the need and capacity to make linkages. Co-management, however, involves a sharing of responsibility and authority between the government and a defined community of local users in the management of a resource. Co-management approaches thus attempt an integration of some of the institutions outlined in previous sections, whereas community-based approaches advocate a reversal of top–down management. Much of the experience in this area concentrates on community-based projects but also observes that these initiatives are often not sustainable in the long run. The lack of long-run stability is a result of the community organizations remaining outside the formal institutions of government. They do not change the legal and governance frameworks controlling use of and access to coastal resources on any level other than the most immediate local scale.

We argue that integrated coastal management requires horizontal and vertical integration within and between formal government organizations and community organizations and informal institutions at different scales if it is to successfully bring about long-term change in coastal resource management. Chapter 3 examines some of the means for bringing about this integration and discusses in particular how deliberative inclusionary processes can be used as bridges between formal and informal institutions, and how transformative processes go beyond a shift from government to community-based management to co-management of the coast.

Chapter 3

Making Choices

Having examined the institutions governing coastal resources, we now turn to a discussion of how institutions and managers make choices about development and conservation strategies. Most decisions about managing coastal resources involve trade-offs between different goods and services, different uses and users. But how are these trade-offs agreed and assessed? Because of the multiple uses and users of coastal zones, successful management strategies invariably need to be based on collective action. This chapter examines some conceptual underpinnings of decision-making and explores how different societal actors are included in these processes.

SOCIETAL TRADE-OFFS IN COASTAL MANAGEMENT

Social science theories of decision-making

Diverse social sciences from anthropology to psychology explore how societies and individuals make choices about allocating scarce resources, to provide an understanding of choices in the face of limited information and uncertain futures. These theories are distinct from each other and are often in conflict about methods, scope and the framing of the questions – ie, whose decisions? Which decisions? Thus the means of decision-making and the outcomes of decision-making, from efficiency, equity and legitimacy perspectives, are all contested concepts. Ultimately, a pluralistic approach to decision-making is justified: given the complexity and the fundamental nature of the decisions being taken about coastal zones, no discipline can have a monopoly on insights. Thus a contextualized and scale-specific examination of the decision-making processes in coastal zones is required. Two important issues in resource allocation are considered here. First, which criteria should we use for choosing among efficient allocations of resources that are equally efficient in economic terms? In other words, how do we determine who should be the main beneficiary from the management of the coastal zone? Second, can decisions made on the basis of the sovereignty of the market and prices ever bring about sustainability (Bromley, 1998)? Related to this issue, are lowest common denominator decisions within a democracy always compatible with making a socially optimal decision about our coastal resources?

Much political research suggests that in any society there are likely to be a wide range of beliefs about how best to allocate resources. Economists have sought to encompass this diversity and collapse it to a simple metric by asking which allocation of resources might maximize social welfare. One of the main conditions for maximizing social welfare is that of 'Pareto optimality'. This assumes that an allocation of resources maximizes social welfare when no one can be made better off without making someone else worse off. Another condition is that the allocation is equitable. 'Equitable' means that no one individual prefers any other individual's allocation of resources to his or her own. Economists say that when a distribution of resources is both Pareto efficient and equitable, it is a 'fair' distribution. However, several questions underpin this theory:

- How can human well-being be defined and measured?
- If measures of human welfare could be accurately determined, would this be adequate information on which to make resource allocation decisions?
- How can welfare gains and losses be aggregated across different individuals?

At a philosophical level, the question remains whether or not choices on behalf of society should be made based on maximizing an aggregation of the preferences of individuals in that society. Underscoring this, is it possible to construct an aggregate – known in economics as a social welfare function – that reflects all individuals' views and preferences? On the basis of the work of Kenneth Arrow, it seems that the answer is 'no' (see Box 3.1).

Arrow's theorem in essence confirms that trade-offs always have to be made in decision-making and that these trade-offs make resource allocation decisions multi-dimensional. For example, in a coastal zone management situation, 50 per cent of the population may believe that conservation should be prioritized whereas 50 per cent may believe that human development should take top priority. Clearly, we cannot assume that, overall, society is indifferent between conservation and development. If a decision were taken on the basis of only one group's preferences, then this would violate one of the axioms set out by Arrow in Box 3.1 – non-dictatorship. In the real world, it is clear that almost no-one is indifferent, and making a fair decision that satisfies the multiple stakeholders with their various interests is very difficult.

The understandings generated from Arrows Impossibility Theorem, coupled with the problems associated with a lack of consensus on which criteria to use in decision-making, highlight the coastal zone management decision-making dilemma. How does one make decisions about common property, state and open access resources when there is no agreement about who should be the beneficiary of the decision or management? And how do you make a decision when there is no consensus among those interested in the decision outcome? These issues both relate to social choice. Together they create one of the fundamental resource allocation questions that we have to consider: how can sustainable, sustained or survivable development by achieved (Pezzey, 1997)?

BOX 3.1 'YOU CAN'T PLEASE ALL THE PEOPLE ALL OF THE TIME'

Kenneth Arrow asked the question: 'Is there a consistent ranking of outcomes from resource allocation on a society-wide scale that fairly records individual preferences?' He developed rules to try to characterize preferences and, since these could not be simultaneously met, Arrow arrived at this now-famous Impossibility Theorem. Arrow devised six conditions for creating a social preference ranking in relation to the ranking of three social states: A, B, and C (these could, for example, refer to an allocation of coastal resources under different property rights regimes).

- The ranking must include all social states (options). Either A is preferred to B, B is preferred to A, or A and B are equally desirable.
- The ranking must be transitive. If A is preferred to B, and B is preferred to C, then A is preferred to C.
- The ranking must be positively related to individual preferences. If A is unanimously preferred to B by both Smith and Jones, then A is preferred to B.
- If a new social state becomes feasible, this fact should not affect the social ranking of the original states. If between A and B, A is preferred to B, then this will remain true if a new state (D) becomes feasible.
- Social preferences should not be imposed, for example by custom. Individual tastes should be reflected.
- The preference relationship should not be dictated by one individual, ie one person's preferences will not determine society's preferences.

The Impossibility Theorem states that if a social decision mechanism satisfies all the above properties, then it can only reflect the preferences of one individual, hence it must be a dictatorship. Arrow therefore showed that these six conditions for social preference ranking are not compatible with each other.

Source: Based on Arrow (1951)

Principles of collective action

Given that there are necessary trade-offs between preferences of individuals, coastal management requires collective action. Collective actions are those taken by a group (either directly or on its behalf through an organization) in pursuit of members' perceived interests, whereby mutual benefits can be gained by individuals cooperating rather than working against each other to achieve an outcome. In coastal management, where resources frequently exist under multiple property rights, there are many different users and limited information about the impacts of different management strategies. In these circumstances collective action is rational and normal.

The interactions between individuals that might lead to collective action are often described using game theory, which is an area of social science that deals with understanding individual decision-making under uncertainty. Interactions in coastal management can be described, for example, as an 'assurance game', in which each actor must be certain of the benefits of contributing to a common cause. Assurance games have been formalized and analysed in various resource

Dive operator / Hotelier	Don't provide clean beach	Provide clean beach
Don't provide sewage treatment	0, 0	0, –8
Provide sewage treatment	–8, 0	4, 4

Figure 3.1 *The benefits of collective action for beach tourist facilities in an assurance game*

management situations, and are reviewed in Sandler (1997) and Runge (1984), for example.

Take the example of a clean beach in a tourist area where there are two businesses, a beach-based recreational dive operation and a hotel. Both the hotelier and the dive operator stand to gain from tourists using the beach on a daily basis. Each business must contribute to the upkeep of the beach to ensure a steady supply of, in this case, financial benefits. The hotel needs to ensure clean water and so must invest in high-grade sewage treatment, while the dive operator must clean the beach of rubbish and provide jetty facilities. Without both of these services, clean water and a clean beach, tourists will stay away. Thus there are incentives for private investment for mutual gain. In Figure 3.1 this example is turned into a 'pay-off matrix', in which the costs and benefits strategies of the hotelier and dive operator are included as hypothetical quantities. Each of the agents incurs costs of eight units (of finance or other costs) for their investment in maintaining the environment. Each receives a benefit of six units from each investment contributed, but neither receives any benefit unless both the hotelier and the dive operator invest in providing the services. In the case that both invest, each receives a net pay-off of four units. For the hotelier this is equal to the benefit of having tourists in a clean environment: 12 units (6 times 2) less the cost incurred by the hotelier (8 units). The same figures apply for the dive operator and both businesses benefit from the collective action.

If just the hotelier or just the dive operator invests in cleaning the beach, they would both lose (see the upper right and lower left boxes) and there would be a net pay-off of minus eight units. This is the free rider problem. But, unlike the common situation in 'prisoner's dilemma' games (see below), the happy situation of both investing in the upkeep of the beach is self-enforcing because if one player cooperates and invests, it is in the interest of the other to do so. So, if the hotelier invests in sewage treatment and hence keeps the water clean, the decision of the dive operator is a choice between not investing (pay-off of zero units) or of investing (pay-off of four units). Runge (1984) and others discuss the other attributes of the assurance game, pointing out the downsides to this apparently desirable situation. These pitfalls include the observation that the top left outcome box in Figure 3.1, where no-one invests, is as stable as the bottom right, the desirable outcome. Nevertheless, there are potential situations where collective action is of mutual benefit in coastal areas. The key is to determine and promote those principles that lead to cooperative action rather than use conflicts. This picture of mutual benefit does not, of course, apply in every resource conflict situation in coastal zones. Sometimes the conflicts are closer to a prisoner's dilemma, in which the stable outcome is detrimental for both parties and for conservation.

How can collective action be promoted and empowered? Some answers come from a decade of empirical research on commons management (for example, Agrawal, 2001; Adger, 2002). From a wealth of data and case studies, success has been hypothesized as the result of a complex interaction of a number of factors: the nature of the resource itself, the technologies of enforcement, the relationships between resources and user groups, the features of the user group, and the relationship between users and the state and legal system.

The motivations and relationships between stakeholders are central to this success. In 1994, on Malekula Island in Vanuatu, the local government council identified the need for locally protected areas. Protected areas were established that were thought to be consistent with local needs and wants in relation to ecosystem conservation (Tacconi, 1997). Participatory approaches were used to determine stakeholders needs. Methods used included: group and individual meetings, analysis of topographic maps, analysis of livelihood sources and development aspirations and options, and surveys of forest, agricultural and marine resources. The final decision was made in agreement with stakeholders to manage land use conflicts through separation of conflicting uses, by delineating the area into zones wherein different activities were allowed. By engaging the stakeholders in the decision-making process, the final decision to separate the conflicting uses was supported by the different stakeholders, and an apparently socially accepted system of protected areas flourished.

Other issues also affect the likelihood of successful collective action (Wade, 1988; Ostrom, 1990; and others). First, the boundaries of the physical resource should be defined. The more clearly defined it is, the greater the chances of successful commons management. Second, if the users are resident at the location of the resource then this increases the chances of success through reducing enforcement costs. Enforcement and other transaction costs are weighed against the benefits from conserving the resource. Third, the greater the demand for the outputs and the reliance on the resource within a livelihood system, the greater the chance of successful common property management. Fourth, the better defined the user group, the greater the chance of success. But conflicts can still occur between small groups of users.

This is not to say that common property regimes are a 'natural' state of affairs for coastal management. Both private and communal property rights can lead to undesirable environmental impacts. The important issue is the management and sustainability of the resources. In defining the circumstances in which common property works best, empirical studies have converged on the factors outlined above and depicted in Figure 3.2. These are the nature of the resource, the nature

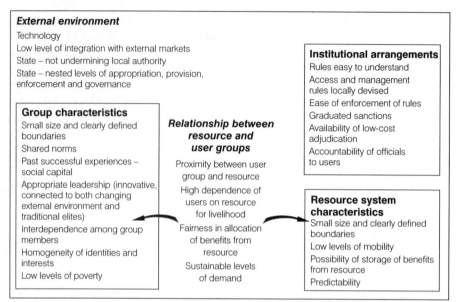

External environment
Technology
Low level of integration with external markets
State – not undermining local authority
State – nested levels of appropriation, provision,
enforcement and governance

Institutional arrangements
Rules easy to understand
Access and management
rules locally devised
Ease of enforcement of rules
Graduated sanctions
Availability of low-cost
adjudication
Accountability of officials
to users

Group characteristics
Small size and clearly defined
boundaries
Shared norms
Past successful experiences –
social capital
Appropriate leadership (innovative,
connected to both changing
external environment and
traditional elites)
Interdependence among group
members
Homogeneity of identities and
interests
Low levels of poverty

***Relationship between
resource and
user groups***
Proximity between user
group and resource
High dependence of
users on resource
for livelihood
Fairness in allocation
of benefits from
resource
Sustainable levels
of demand

**Resource system
characteristics**
Small size and clearly defined
boundaries
Low levels of mobility
Possibility of storage of benefits
from resource
Predictability

Source: Adapted from Agrawal (2001)

Figure 3.2 *Enabling conditions for sustainable collective management of coastal
and other resources*

of the group, the institutional arrangements for management and external factors affecting the political nature of the interactions, often termed 'the political ecology of resource use' (Brown and Rosendo, 2000).

A key aspect of coastal zone management relates to the role of the state in enforcing the legal framework for use: whether there is a divergence between de facto and de jure property rights. The de facto property rights are those that are observed to be actually in operation and hence affect resource allocation and individual decisions. De jure property rights constitute explicit legal ownership, trade and use rights as determined by the state, but are only consistent with de facto property rights to the extent that they are enforced. Thus under the 'property rights school', which promotes private property as a solution to sustainable management, it is the divergence of de jure and de facto rights that causes unsustainable use. It is clear that de jure rights are not a necessary condition for the existence of sustainable common property management, but the legal framework of property rights can be used to promote security and stability among resource users.

Common property management regimes are 'a set of institutional arrangements that define the conditions of access to a range of benefits arising from collectively used natural resources' (Swallow and Bromley, 1995). The administrative systems may be centralized (for example, a village fishery committee) or a diffuse set of actors, depending on historical and cultural factors. The underlying conditions determining the nature of the institutions undertaking management are not static. They evolve to incorporate external political situations and natural changes in the resource itself.

For example, when the crayfish of the Racken watershed in Sweden became scarce, the community fisheries organization became largely moribund. When the conservation of the remaining stock became a priority, the benefits of resurrecting the traditional management were realized (Olsson and Folke, 2001). The state and traditional regulation of oyster fishing and farming in Zeeland province in the Netherlands was successful through the 19th century. In 1903 there was a European-wide 'oyster scare' when typhoid, transmitted through the bivalves from sewage effluent, resulted in the deaths of consumers in England. In Zeeland the turmoil of collapsing markets and lack of trust from consumers led to bankruptcies and an overhaul of management institutions, from central government to the local fisheries committees (detailed in a fascinating account by Van Ginkel, 1996; 1999). Both the Swedish and the Netherlands examples demonstrate that institutions are not static. They strive to manage resources for their own and for the collective good. Yet they co-evolve with changing market and political circumstances and with natural and human-induced resource dynamics.

There is no blueprint for a stable or successful set of institutions for the management of common pool resources. Examples abound in which private property rights have been allocated but management has not been supported because local stakeholders' interests have not been considered (see Baland and Platteau, 1996; Agrawal and Gibson, 1999; Clague, 1997). Many empirical studies note that the top–down allocation of property rights alone is not adequate to prevent resource degradation in common pool resources. There is an increasing recognition of complex and hybrid systems of property rights for natural resource management. Practice and theory are co-evolving phenomena in this area. The 'rolling back' or 'hollowing out' of the state in the 1980s and 1990s has resulted in a divergent set of property rights for many coastal resources, particularly in developing countries. In some cases there has been a spontaneous reassertion of traditional ways of managing resources, for example, in fisheries management. In other cases there have been systematic experiments with planned co-management partnerships for common coastal resources. But the most consistent set of property rights changes in the natural resource area have been towards the private allocation of rights, sometimes backed up by market-based tradeable property rights.

In fisheries, for example, while some countries have implemented efficiency-gaining private property rights for fisheries catch, other areas have seen the necessary evolution of local management in the absence of the state. Ruddle (1998) and others have demonstrated the historical persistence of the *van chai* village fisheries system in Vietnam, whereby the local ancestral shrines in villages laid down the rules for fishing, including acceptable technologies, profit sharing and dispute conciliation. Ruddle (1998) also charts the re-emergence of the *van chai* system in the 1990s, which was associated with a reduction in state planning (see also Thorburn, 2000). For other coastal resources, White and others (1994) demonstrate a range of co-management solutions to coral reef management. Where the state has been ineffective in preventing overuse, the sharing of rights with local users can, in particular circumstances, lead to more sustainable management outcomes (see also Box 3.2).

Box 3.2 The Norwegian fisheries experience

The Lofoten fishery in Norway is an example of a longstanding, successful co-management venture. In 1897, the Norwegian government enacted special legislation that delegated the responsibility for regulating the fishery to the fishermen themselves. The law was enacted in response to the problems of overcrowding and gear conflicts caused by numerous users competing for fishing space and fish. The law contained regulations for the organization of the fishers. When the fishers organized themselves they developed the rules for the management of the fishery. The rules they established were that regulatory committees were to be established, the members of which were to be elected by and from the boat captains. The fishery regulations that the committee established included: allowable fishing time, the type of fishing gear that could be used, and how much space would be reserved for each type of gear. The Lofoten fishery co-management arrangement continues to ensure that order is kept on the fishing grounds today.

Source: Lim and others (1995)

In Chile, New Zealand and other countries, an individual transferable quota system has replaced state regulation of fisheries take (for example, Hughey and others, 2000; Peña-Torres, 1997) to promote sustainable harvesting. Evidence suggests, however, that privatization is not a panacea for overfishing.

Communities and social capital

In addition to the institutions of governance and their rules, community is the most important ingredient for collective management (Taylor, 1998). Informed and empowered communities can create the environment for voluntary action to provide social order, resolve conflicts and regulate common resources. If hybrid co-management between governments and communities is to succeed, then it must mobilize and foster cooperative relations among the stakeholders, while 'the hierarchical relations between governors and governed must themselves be characterized by long-term repeated interactions, cooperation, reciprocity and trust' (Taylor, 1998, p252; see also Taylor, 1996).

Neither co-management nor the emergence of collective action are ever simply spontaneous phenomena. Governments, agencies of governments and private resource owners do not easily give up their vested interests and power bases. So why is co-management of resources, particularly in fisheries and marine protected areas, so popular? For governments, the reason is often that of reducing the costs of governing – allocating rights and responsibilities to other stakeholders can reduce the transactions costs of management – rather than any notions of empowerment or reducing democratic deficits. Singleton (2000) has shown in the context of the Pacific north-west salmon fishery in the USA, however, that co-management, if successful, is as resource-intensive as traditional top–down management. Further, co-management does not guarantee sustainable management or the elimination of conflicts between states and communities over resources. There is often uncritical acceptance that the participation of all stakeholders is the key to the sustainable management of natural resources. This tenet is questioned from a variety of perspectives. The diversity of interests within the communities involved in resource management, and the wider democratic framework within which such management occurs, mean that, in effect, community management is not always best (Hayward, 1995).

Social capital is made up of 'the norms and networks that enable people to act collectively' (Woolcock and Narayan, 2000). These networks are scale-dependent and exist both outside the state and between the state and other elements of society. Social capital is associated with a progressive and perhaps flexible and adaptive society. It is a necessary glue for social resilience, but also for economic development (Adger, 2000). Different types of social capital, however, are important at different times to different social groups. Social capital is made up of the sharing of knowledge, financial risk and market information, or claims for reciprocity in times of crisis. Ties within a defined socio-economic group have come to be known as 'bonding' social capital and may be based on family kinship and locality. By contrast, 'networking' (or 'bridging') social capital is made up of the economic and other ties that are external to social groups.

Networking social capital tends to be based less on friendship and kinship than on the weaker bonds of trust and reciprocity. Hence it has fewer formal collective-action rules of enforcement and sanction and becomes increasingly reliant on legal and formal institutions. Putnam and others (1993) argue that the relative economic performance of regions in Italy in the preceding decades could be attributed to the density of social capital. This they measured by examining regional historical records of participation in civil society institutions such as churches and political parties. In effect, they examined the presence of networking social capital and, to a lesser degree, bonding social capital, and argued that this played a part in explaining regional differences in economic growth, employment levels and other economic indicators. Importantly, social capital emerges in society for reasons other than to promote development: there can be many reasons for the emergence of collective action. The hotelier and the dive operator in the earlier example may choose to cooperate to keep the beach clean because their families use the beach at the weekend. Thus social capital and collective action emerge in diverse social and market circumstances.

Can social capital be encouraged for inclusionary coastal management by governments? An institutional view of social capital argues that 'the very capacity of social groups to act in their collective interest depends on the quality of the formal institutions under which they reside' (Woolcock and Narayan, 2000, p234). Clearly, the roles of government in encouraging the development of social capital and local institutions are intertwined. A set of potential interactions between networks and the state is shown in Figure 3.3, building on the ideas of Woolcock and Narayan (2000). There are some types of coastal management (for example, the provision of large-scale infrastructure) which are only easily realizable by the state. Figure 3.3 shows that, with a well-functioning state, the state can provide the necessary underpinning and social security for all social groups (left). The ideal situation is a synergy between state and civil society (Evans, 1996) that promotes social and policy learning (upper right). Social

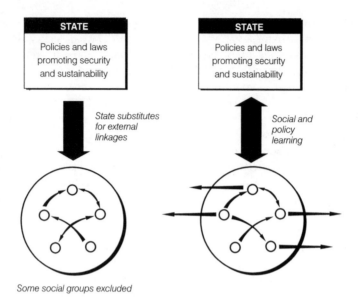

Figure 3.3 *Bonding and networking social capital and vertical linkages between state and society with a well-functioning state*

learning comes about through collective activities such as discourse, imitation and conflict resolution.

An example of the situation portrayed in Figure 3.3 is the need for legitimacy in partnerships in planning for coastal defence. In the UK, inclusionary and participatory planning processes are novel but increasingly utilized when long-term decisions on management require vested interests to be subjugated. O'Riordan (2001) and O'Riordan and Ward (1997) report on the building of trust between local stakeholders and government agencies in planning for the East Anglian coast. In this case, nature conservation organizations and local economic interests came to a compromise in designing coastal protection schemes. Social learning in this case came about through the widespread recognition and validation of differential perceptions of risk by local stakeholders.

Figure 3.4 illustrates the undesirable circumstances in which social capital is not allowed to function (left) or is the only means of survival (right). When a state is driven by ideology, subjected to colonialism or provoked by other circumstances to be in conflict with civil society, conflict ensues and the most marginal sections of society are made vulnerable. In these circumstances civil strife and population displacement can occur, sometimes triggering famine even in the absence of a fall in food production or an environmental catastrophe. This situation explains some of the major natural and unnatural disasters of the 20th century (Adger and Brooks, 2002).

The practice of resource management in many areas appears, in effect, to be running ahead of theory. But how local and how community-oriented does

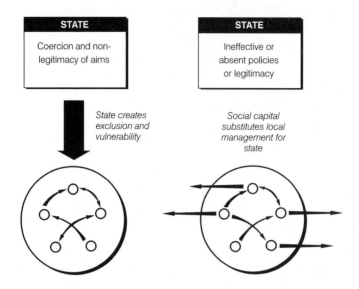

Figure 3.4 *Bonding and networking social capital and vertical linkages between state and society in the absence of a functioning state*

successful management have to be? Are there limits to participatory management in terms of complexity or geographical area? The factors that determine whether participatory management can exist and flourish appar to be scale-dependent (Tompkins and others, 2002). The density of networks and the ability to combine information and resources outside the local spheres of institutions are important means by which participatory processes are maintained.

Cox (1998) and others argue that these networks between institutions, or sets of interactions between individuals and groups, are in fact distinguished by this scale characteristic. Social relations and interactions that cannot be undertaken other than locally and which are 'relied on for the realization of essential interests' can be defined as 'spaces of dependence' (Cox, 1998). Institutions organize themselves to secure their existence and in doing so create networks at other levels: in the media, in other areas of political life or even internationally. These networks can be defined as 'spaces of engagement'. The importance of the classification of networks of social capital in Table 3.1 can be seen in participatory resource management. The greater the depth of networks of engagement, the greater the opportunities should be for social learning and the widespread adoption of new institutional forms. But spaces of dependence are equally important in defining the winners and losers in any resource allocation. Examples of the localized spaces of dependence and spaces of exchange for the institutions surrounding participatory natural resource management are outlined in Table 3.1. These show that operational arrangements generally exist at smaller spatial scales, while constitutional arrangements are often observed primarily at the national

Table 3.1 *Networks for participatory natural resource management*

	Spaces of dependence	Spaces of engagement
Constitutional arrangements	Often national-level laws and socially sanctioned norms	Often international laws and pressures from international organizations
Institutional structures	Budgetary and other regulatory functions	Cross-department initiatives in government. Use of media and co-opting of associations and interest groups
Operational arrangements	Local organizations such as councils and local government as well as interest groups, associations and other outlets	Contacts with national and international media, campaigning groups and information

Source: Tompkins and others (2002)

level. For all groups the spaces of exchange can expand the spatial scale upwards, even to international and global levels. Thus integrating local insights and knowledge into coastal management is not simply a matter of dealing with people and organizations in one locality. Networks and social capital extend far beyond the location of coastal conflicts. And local-level institutions will always be constrained by governments, rules and the necessities of local economic forces.

INCLUSION IN COASTAL MANAGEMENT

Everything we have highlighted so far in this chapter indicates that the inclusion of key institutions, actors and stakeholders is a critical factor in the successful management of natural resources. But as we have already seen, there are many different ways of bringing about inclusion. We need to ask two key questions: Who is being included? And, what are they being included in?

Stakeholders and participation

Coastal stakeholders include the obvious coastal residents and extractive users, indirect users of coastal goods and services, coastal visitors and many others. Many coastal stakeholders are not aware of their influence over the demand for coastal goods and services, or the supply of damaging inputs that they provide. For example, inland residents who own small aquariums; package tourists or independent travellers to coastal areas; people who eat fish or marine animal meals at restaurants worldwide; consumers of bath sponges, mother-of-pearl or black coral jewellery; and beachcombers who collect stones and shells all influence the demand for coastal resources. Many of these stakeholders also influence the supply. Managing this vast, diverse group of coastal stakeholders is a central problem for coastal management agencies.

Table 3.2 *A typology of coastal actors and interests on a macro-to-micro continuum*

Continuum level	Example stakeholders	Environmental interests
Global and international wider society	International agencies, foreign governments, environmental lobbies, future generations	Biodiversity conservation, climatic regulation
National	National governments, macro planners, urban pressure groups, NGOs	Fisheries, tourism development, resource and biodiversity protection
Regional	Fisheries departments, regional authorities, coastal communities	Fisheries productivity, water supply protection
Local off-site	Fishers, employees in tourism, local tradespeople	Access to amenities, beaches, mangroves, conflict avoidance
Local on-site	Residents	Land for habitation, range of marine and coastal products, cultural sites

Research in the field of participatory resource management and community-based resource management suggests that the engagement of stakeholders in decisions about how the coast is managed or in the management itself is a useful start. However, knowing who to engage is not easy, as the boundaries between stakeholders and even the definition of the term 'stakeholder' have evolved and changed over time. When the focus of management was on the application of property rights and the exclusion of groups of users from parts of the coastal zone, stakeholders were very narrowly defined as people who lived or worked in the coastal zone. Research on the identification of stakeholders has generated a range of definitions and meanings for the term 'stakeholder' that are more inclusive than past definitions. For example, Grimble and others (1994) suggest that stakeholders are a diverse group that exist at many scales, not just the local level. A similar typology can be applied to coastal stakeholders at different scales on a micro- to macro-continuum. The example shows that stakeholders are not just the local users of the resources (see Table 3.2).

Using the concept of scale as the defining characteristic of different stakeholder groups can uncover an enormous number of groups and individuals who could be considered stakeholders in an initial scoping exercise. However, in developing participatory or inclusive approaches it is also important to determine the extent to which different stakeholders are to be included.

Participation or inclusion in coastal zone management can exist in many forms, and there are many different levels of inclusion. At the most basic level participation can be passive consultation, where information is disseminated and those impacted are informed of future plans. At its most active, participation involves people and communities in sharing power and actual management. Table 3.3 is a typology of participation that shows the possible range of participation in coastal zone management.

Table 3.3 *A typology of participation in coastal zone management*

Forms of participation	Characteristics of each type of participation
Passive participation	People are told what is going to happen or has already happened. There is no mechanism to respond to suggestions made by stakeholders. The information generated and shared belongs to management.
Participation in information giving	People participate by answering questions posed by the decision-makers using questionnaire surveys or similar approaches. No opportunity exists for stakeholders to influence proceedings. The information generated is neither shared nor checked for accuracy.
Participation by consultation	Stakeholders are consulted and external agents listen to the views expressed. These external agents define both problems and solutions. They may modify these in light of stakeholders' responses. Consultative processes do not offer any partnership in decision-making and decision-makers are not obliged to take stakeholders' views on board.
Participation for material incentives	People participate in return for food, cash or other material incentives. This is called 'participation', yet those involved have no stake in prolonging activities when the incentives end.
Functional participation	People participate by forming groups to meet predetermined objectives, often promoted by external groups. Such involvement does not tend to be at early stages of project cycles or planning, but rather after major decisions have been made. The institutions created tend to be dependent on external assistance, but may become independent in time.
Interactive participation	People participate with decision-makers in joint analysis that leads to the creation of new local groups or the strengthening of existing ones. These groups take control over local decisions so that people have a stake in maintaining structures or practices. It tends to involve interdisciplinary methods and structured learning processes.
Self-mobilization/ active participation	People participate by taking initiatives independent of external institutions to change systems. Such self-initiated mobilization and collective action may or may not challenge existing distributions of land, assets and power.

Source: Pimbert and Pretty (1994)

The level of participation depends on the degree of control decision-makers in the formal institutions hold over the resource in question, and the amount of decision-making power they are willing to give up. The answer to finding a balance between formal and informal institutional involvement in resource management often depends solely on how the decision-makers with power perceive the other stakeholders. The stakeholders may be perceived either as a threat to the success of a decision, or as possible owners of the decision, or as co-managers of a resource. Figure 3.5 takes fisheries management as an example

Rock Lobster Industry Council *(New Zealand)*	Village multi-sector cooperatives *(Japan)*	Lake Titicaca *(Peru)*
British Columbia halibut fishery *(Canada)*	Guardians of Fiordland Fisheries *(New Zealand)*	Reef management by clan chiefs *(South Pacific)*
	Torres Strait Fisheries Management Committee *(Australia)*	

INCREASING LEVELS OF SELF-GOVERNMENT

Advisory management	**Co-management**	**Self-management**
Government agencies facilitate most aspects of management and set rules in consultation with fisheries stakeholders	Equal sharing of power and decision-making responsibility between government and stakeholders	Fishers decide on own operating regime but within a framework established by government applying to all fisheries

Advisory management:
- Government-funded
- Government-managed and facilitated
- Reliant on government compliance
- Lobbying by stakeholders to increase influence

Co-management:
- Largely government-funded
- Shared management and facilitation
- Largely reliant on government compliance
- Seeking shared management

Self-management:
- Self-funded
- Self-managed and facilitated
- Largely self-compliant
- Seeking autonomy and self-control

Source: Adapted from hughey et al (2000)

Figure 3.5 *Forms of advisory and cooperative management in fisheries*

and shows how different forms of participation translate into forms of self-management, co-management and advisory management in different approaches. Self-management represents the most active form of stakeholder mobilization, whereas advisory management is a passive form of consultation, where government continues to make all key decisions and controls funding.

Evidence suggests that community-based resource management (or participatory resource management) can increase effectiveness. If communities or important stakeholders are committed to making a community-based resource management programme work, the programme stands more chance of success than if it were not supported. Conversely, a lack of participation by all important stakeholders in decision-making processes is widely recognized as an important factor in generating additional conflict between those included in and those excluded from the decision-making process. Where important stakeholders are excluded, decisions are likely to reach stalemate or to fail in implementation, as is the case with fisheries management in Thailand.

In Trang Province, Thailand, fishers frustrated by the intrusion of trawlers and large 'push net' boats into near-shore waters worked with a local NGO to lobby the government to enforce the existing laws, which banned all fishing within 3km of the shore. The success of this initiative led to the development of a federation of fishers, which has continued to campaign for better law enforcement by government. However, the success of the fishers has been countered by the continued rapid development of the shoreline by developers and an increase in land-based sources of pollution. The lack of inclusion of the important private sector developers in the federation of fishers is considered to be a constraint to its effectiveness (Sudara, 1999).

The mechanisms by which the different stakeholders can engage in coastal zone management are various and may be termed 'deliberative inclusionary processes'. As the previous examples show, stakeholders themselves can join forces in some form of informal institution or collective action, such as co-management or community-based resource management. Alternatively, stakeholders – even without support from government – can develop social capital to expand their networks of engagement or create new social institutions for management.

Deliberative inclusionary processes

What, then, are the processes by which different actors or stakeholders are able to participate in aspects of coastal management? The term deliberative inclusionary processes (DIPs) covers a range of participatory policy-making processes, management practices and community empowering actions. These processes are variously applied as a means of better and more effectively implementing policy, to redistribute power and benefits, and as part of efforts to bring about deliberative democratic approaches to environmental decision-making. DIPs have been applied in many different economic, political and cultural contexts worldwide. Holmes and Scoones (2000) provide a review of DIPs in developed and developing countries. Box 3.3 outlines some of the various objectives of DIPs. The objectives will clearly change according to context, site and issue.

There are two key features that distinguish DIPs: deliberation and inclusion. 'Deliberation' means careful consideration or discussion. Decision-making and planning thus require social interaction and debate. Deliberation implies that the different positions of stakeholders are recognized and respected. Participants are expected to reflect on, evaluate and re-evaluate their own and others' positions, and the process of deliberation aims to bring about some kind of transformation of values or preferences and to foster negotiation between participants in order to reach a decision. 'Inclusion' is the action of including different participants in these processes. Clearly, who to include is critical in these processes; this is further discussed in Chapter 4.

An array of procedural techniques, mechanisms and methods have developed under the broad umbrella of DIPs. These include, for example, citizens' juries, focus groups, issue forums, participatory rural appraisal, visioning exercises and various types of workshops and working groups. Box 3.4 outlines some of the main forms of DIPs applied to environmental planning and decision-making. Typical principles adopted by these methods are: working with small groups of people; focusing on the future and on common ground; urging full attendance and participation; incorporating the widest possible range of interests; and seeking public commitments to action (Holmes and Scoones, 2000). Once more, it is evident that different DIPs reflect the range of forms of participation found in Table 3.3. In developing countries, DIPs have been associated with the rhetoric of participation and empowerment and, in the North, with democracy and representation. The notion of community is often at the heart of DIPs, and so these methods are often linked to community-

---

Box 3.3 Objectives of deliberative and inclusionary processes

Educative

Civic deliberation is seen as a means of encouraging political learning about an issue or a problem. This might range from simply providing individuals with more information or knowledge to the expectation that as a result of this deliberation citizens can make collective judgements and participate in decision-making in the future.

Consensual

This stresses the procedures by which participants can come to a common agreement on an issue, or over future courses of action. There is a desire to find common ground on an issue. Participants may recognize that consensus is possible, and so seek compromise – 'I can live with that'-type resolutions.

Instrumental

This approach perceives direct political or legislative results as the purpose of democratic deliberation. Procedures may be organized around the communication of established political interests. Deliberative sessions can be judged in terms of effectiveness, efficiency and influence and might result in the development, improvement or blocking of a proposal.

Conflictual

This attempts to give the widest possible space to the expression and development of individual points of view so that the primary focus is on unrestricted discourse. The results may be educative but may also serve as a basis for future decision-making.

Source: Adapted from Holmes and Scoones (2000)

---

based initiatives as outlined in Chapter 2 and further discussed below. The recognition of diverse values and lay knowledge are also of fundamental importance to how these processes operate. A key feature of DIPs, however, is their use to link government agencies and civil society groups in co-management strategies for natural resource management. In many instances, DIPs are used as instruments of local government through initiatives such as Agenda 21. In one respect, then, DIPs are the mechanisms by which the formal and informal institutions of coastal management described in Chapter 2 can be linked; DIPs are used to form bridges between these spheres of decision-making and management.

Experience on rigorously evaluating the outcomes of DIPs in various contexts is only recently emerging (for example, Spash, 2001) along with a much more critical approach to participation (see Cooke and Kothari, 2001; Few, 2001). Issues raised include the extent to which the utilization of DIPs reflects any meaningful devolution of power to civil society and also their representativeness, accountability and political and ethical legitimacy (O'Neill,

Box 3.4 Different forms of deliberative and inclusionary processes in environmental decision-making management and planning

Citizens' juries

A group of citizens is brought together to consider a particular issue, usually set by the local authority. They may receive evidence from expert witnesses and cross-questioning may occur. The process may last days, and at the end a report is drawn up setting out the views of the jury, including any significant differences. Juries' views inform decision-making.

Consensus conferences

A panel of lay people develops its understanding of a technical or scientific issue in dialogue with experts. The panel normally consists of 10–20 volunteers. It meets over a series of days, questions experts and has open public meetings.

Focus groups

One-off focus groups may be convened in a similar manner to citizens' juries. Views are sought on a particular subject, which may be a specific local issue or a broader policy or strategy. In the past, focus groups have been used extensively in market research and also in political processes for refining and testing policy. Focus groups generally last just a few hours, do not question experts and involve around 12 people.

Participatory rural appraisal/participatory research and action

A suite of approaches and methods designed to enable poor people to express and analyse the realities of their lives and conditions, and to plan, monitor and evaluate their actions. Outsiders act as catalysts for local people to decide what information they need and how it will be used.

Rapid rural appraisal

Closely related to participatory rural appraisal, this involves data collection by outsiders through techniques such as participant observation, structured interviews and visual techniques.

Visioning exercises

A range of methods (including focus groups) used to establish a 'vision' for the future, which may be a broad strategy for a locality or have a more specific focus – for example, the environmental consultations for Agenda 21.

Multi-criteria mapping

Attempts to combine transparency of numerical approaches with deliberative constructivist approaches.

Source: Adapted from Holmes and Scoones (2000) and O'Riordan (2000)

2001). We reflect on this issue and its implications for inclusive approaches to coastal management in later chapters.

CONCLUSIONS: INCLUSIVE COASTAL MANAGEMENT

In summary, social capital and the networks between individuals, groups and the state represent the primary drivers of collective action for coastal management. There are clearly important relationships between community, identity and the politics of resource management. In some instances governments are blind to the needs of coastal communities. They override their social organization in pursuit of the goals of economic development and modernization (Scott, 1998). In these cases local collective action is often in the form of resistance to larger external forces: resistance to port development, to coastal aquaculture (for example, Martinez-Alier, 2001) or to the imposition of fishing restrictions and marine reserves. When social capital evolves in harmony with government, new property regimes and novel institutions can lead to empowering and sustainable management of the coast.

An element of the insights into institutions that we develop in this book concerns the property rights regimes inherent in collective management of the coast. Choosing between property regimes and ways of managing resources is about deciding which interests are to be defended, which costs will be invoked and whose interests are to be developed and sustained (Vatn, 2001). For the ever-increasing proportion of the world's population that relies on a sustained flow of goods and services from the world's coastal seas and margins, there is much at stake. Facilitating inclusionary decision-making structures helps to realize the ambitious goals of sustainable development. It is best brought about through the co-management of resources maintaining and promoting ecosystem resilience, such that stakeholders from civil society buy into a shared vision of sustainable resource management in the long run.

Chapter 4

Tools for Integration

How do we operationalize and implement integration and inclusion in coastal zone management? This and the following two chapters outline some principles and techniques for decision-making to support integrated and inclusionary management and its institutional dimensions. This hybrid set of techniques and procedures is brought together as trade-off analysis. Current coastal zone management practices are evolving, learning from past successes and failures. At a conceptual level it is clear that macro-institutional structures, operational behaviour of management organizations and the informal institutions of collective behaviour must be taken into account at all stages of management to ensure integration and inclusion. Indeed, the importance of adopting integrated and inclusive policy is a recurrent theme in modern coastal zone management. But few operational tools bring together human systems and ecological systems, or manage qualitative and quantitative data simultaneously. The trade-off analysis approach tackles these dilemmas by supporting decisions based on principles of inclusion, integration and legitimacy.

COASTAL ZONE DECISION-MAKING AND THE ROLE OF DECISION-SUPPORT TOOLS

Decisions, decisions

Traditional conceptions of decision analysis characterize the processes of decision-making as having three steps. First, identify the problem. Second, establish the possible courses of action. Third, select a course of action from the choices available (Janssen, 1994). Underlying these steps, it is recognized that decisions are made according to the preferences of the decision-maker and that decisions may not be based on clearly defined objectives: the preferences of decision-makers are implicit rather than explicit, and are usually embedded in the subconscious. For example, a decision-maker may subconsciously place more value on maintaining human-made infrastructure that exists in the coastal zone than on conserving biodiversity. Hence when establishing possible courses of action, the decision-maker may not even consider one possibility (that supports conservation at the expense of human constructions) from the set of choices available. Decisions based on the undeclared, and possibly unknown, preferences of decision-makers are often unsupported (see, for example, Box 3.4 in Chapter 3). Decision-support tools can enable decision-making processes to be both more transparent and more inclusive.

Decision-support tools generate information about the decision problem, generate solutions or alternatives to the problem, and provide an explanation of the structure and content of the decision. They should also ideally identify the different stakeholders as well as their roles and functions in the decision problem. We argue that complex coastal management dilemmas require a mix of techniques appropriate to the context and issues at stake. Comprehensive decision-support tools therefore should include several key components:

- an understanding of the decision problem, including an assessment of the stakeholders, institutions and varied interests in the resource;
- information about the possible alternative options available to the decision-maker;
- information about the impacts of those alternatives on the different stakeholders' interests; and
- an understanding of different stakeholders' preferences for the distribution of costs and benefits from any decision.

Pearce and Markandya (1989) have reviewed the advantages and disadvantages of some of these decision-support tools. As shown in Table 4.1, decision-support tools and aids include cost–benefit analysis, cost-effectiveness analysis, multiple criteria analysis, risk analysis, decision analysis and environmental impact assessment (EIA). Cost–benefit analysis can be effective when used as the sole decision-making tool if the objective is to find the most economically efficient decision. When other issues are important, such as the social distribution of costs and benefits, or where there are multiple objectives for management, other decision-support tools such as multi-criteria analysis are more appropriate. In reality, all decisions on coastal management have consequences for efficiency of resource use, impacts on equity and on externally imposed objectives, and depend on the legitimacy of the institutions implementing the decisions. Explicit decisions assessed using diverse methods and tools are the norm.

Dealing with complexity

Management decisions about coastal zones are made in the face of uncertainty about their outcomes, and hence there are risks attached. Coastal resources are, as we have shown, multiple-use resources; there are conflicting objectives, such as tourism and extractive fishing. Making a decision in circumstances of uncertainty, risk and conflict is often fraught with difficulty: frequently, the easiest decision is to avoid change and promote the status quo. Furthermore, multiple-use resources are seldom managed by a single decision-maker. A wide range of actors is concerned with the day-to-day management of different coastal components, and overall strategic planning is often divided between different government agencies and departments, as shown in Chapter 3.

Table 4.1 *Advantages and disadvantages of a range of decision-support techniques*

Conceptual basis/method	Description	Advantages	Disadvantages
1 Cost-benefit analysis	Evaluates options by quantifying net benefits (benefits minus costs).	• Considers the benefits and costs of management options; • translates all outcomes into commensurate monetary terms; • reveals the most efficient option.	• No direct consideration of the equity distribution of the costs and benefits; • ignores non-quantifiable costs and benefits; • assumes that all stakeholders have equal incomes and levels of well-being.
2 Cost-effectiveness analysis	The least-cost option that meets the goals of the decision-maker is preferred.	• No need to estimate the benefits of different management options; • cost information is often readily available	• The relative importance of outputs is not considered; • no consideration given to the social costs resulting from side-effects of different options.
3 Multi-criteria analysis	Uses mathematical programming techniques to select options based on objective functions with explicit weights of stakeholders applied.	• Allows quantification of implicit costs; • permits the prioritization of options; • the model can reflect multiple goals or objectives for the resources.	• Is an unrealistic characterization of decision-making; • theoretical difficulties associated with aggregating preferences for use as weights in the model; • large information needs.
4 Risk-benefit analysis	Evaluates benefits associated with a policy in comparison with its risks.	• Framework is flexible; • permits consideration of all risks (benefits and costs); • there is no automatic decision rule.	• The framework is too vague; • factors considered to be commensurate are not.
5 Decision analysis	A step-by-step analysis of the consequences of choices under uncertainty.	• The model can reflect multiple goals or objectives for the resources; • the choices to be made are explicit; • there is an explicit recognition of uncertainty.	• The objectives are not always clear; • there is no clear mechanism for assigning weights.
6 Environmental impact assessment	Provides a detailed economic, social and environmental statement of the impacts of management options.	• Requires explicit consideration of environmental effects; • benefits and costs do not have to be monetized.	• Difficult to integrate descriptive and qualitative analyses with monetary costs and benefits; • no clear criteria for using information in the decision-making process.

Source: Adapted from Pearce and Markandya (1989)

Coastal ecosystems and the institutional environment in which coastal zone decisions are made are both difficult to conceptualize due to their multiple layers and actors. Large, dynamic, linked and interdependent ecosystems amplify the challenge of managing the coastal zone.

For small island nations in particular, there is a close interaction between water resources, land use and the coastal environment. Degradation is likely to impact on the sustainability of livelihoods of local populations and the long term viability of any development strategy, including tourism. Boersma and Parrish (1999) argue that marine protected areas (MPAs), for example, often lack functional boundaries and this makes development controls difficult to implement. Land use change in areas adjacent to MPAs leads directly to changes in nutrient loading, which affects the quality and productivity of the marine environment, often in unpredictable ways (Rawlins and others, 1998). Simultaneously, the dependence of coastal communities on fisheries and other marine resources provides direct feedback to land-based livelihood strategies (for example, Andersson and Ngazi, 1998). Thus the ecological and economic systems have linkages often with direct and immediate feedbacks (Berkes and Folke, 1998). The degradation of coastal areas can lead to both a decline in overall tourist revenue with knock-on consequences for local economies, and to impacts on food systems (Dixon and others, 1993; Ruitenbeek and Cartier, 1999). These linkages and feedbacks require interrogation and assessment to inform decision-making, and the trade-offs between ecological, social and economic impacts need to be evaluated.

Coastal managers tend to react to environmental and social change and pressure rather than acting in proactive ways. This is primarily a function of not being able to handle uncertainty in the coastal system. At their very simplest, decision-support tools provide information in a structured framework and allow the sensitivities of the possible outcomes to be explored, thereby overcoming the tendency towards a conservative reaction.

The ecological complexity and multiple uses of many MPAs are compounded by diverse and complex systems of property rights, which require state, private and collective decision-making, and by diverse and often-conflicting users. The unique feature of these multiple-use resources, as argued by Steins and Edwards (1998) and Edwards and Steins (1998), is the important role of 'umbrella' regulations in governing the resource. Thus an important step in the process is the identification of stakeholder groups and the quantification of the impacts of their use in a way that accommodates multiple-user groups and effective intervention by state institutions and regulators, who designate such areas.

ENGAGING STAKEHOLDERS IN DECISION-MAKING

In earlier chapters, it was argued that management for multiple objectives in the coastal zone is less effective when key stakeholders are excluded from decision-making and management. Hence, any decision-support tool must consider the stakeholders involved. Such a consideration usually begins with a stakeholder analysis, and an exploration of the concept of stakeholder. In the management sciences literature a stakeholder is a person, organization or group with an interest in an issue or resource. Stakeholders include both people with power to control the use and management of the resource, and those with no power or influence whose livelihoods are affected by the changing use or management of the resource. Stakeholders vary in the degree of influence and importance they have, and they can be broadly categorized according to whether they have relatively more or less influence or importance with regard to the success of coastal zone management.

Stakeholder analysis is a system for collecting information about groups or individuals who are affected by decisions, categorizing that information and explaining the possible conflicts that may exist between important groups, and areas where trade-offs may be possible. It can be undertaken simply to identify stakeholders, to manage stakeholders and their interests or to explore opportunities for getting groups or individuals to work together. In a stakeholder analysis, the stakeholder groups are often described by socio-economic classifications such as income level, occupational group and employment status, or by their degree of formal involvement in the decision-making processes, group cohesion and formal or informal structures. Stakeholder identification is often complicated by the fact that individual stakeholders tend to fall into more than one category. Finding the right balance of stakeholders and interests is very important, yet ensuring that the right balance is found and maintained is difficult.

In this chapter we begin to explore the usefulness of trade-off analysis and its components in theory and in practice. Much of the practice is outlined in the following chapter with reference to the example of Buccoo Reef Marine Park (BRMP) in Tobago in the West Indies (see Figure 4.1). This established marine park is a prime example of a multiple-use coastal management problem where novel management and intervention through the 1990s have helped to build resilience in both social and natural systems. Background on the context of BRMP is given in Box 4.1, and the major settlements and areas of conflict are shown in Figure 4.2.

Identifying stakeholders

Identifying stakeholders marks the beginning of the formal stakeholder analysis process, and it is the first step towards successful conflict management and consensus building. Behind any stakeholder analysis is the question: who has a legitimate claim on the attention of managers and should therefore be considered a stakeholder? Many forms of stakeholder analysis rely on the subjective assessment of the stakeholders by the decision-maker, the coastal zone manager or the resource users themselves. Hence, it is quite possible that some stakeholder groups will be excluded through ignorance or deliberate exclusion on the part of the identifier.

One method for identifying stakeholders is to use a continuum of stakeholders from the macro-to-micro level, as shown in Table 3.1. This typology is general and so can be applied to other natural resources, and to a

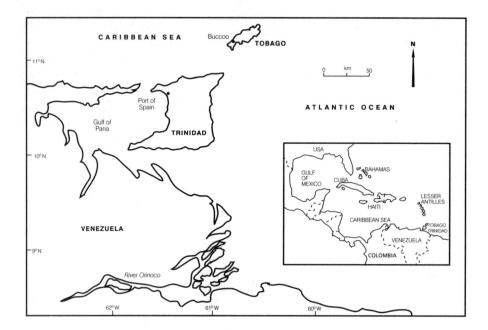

Figure 4.1 *The wider Caribbean and Trinidad and Tobago*

variety of settings. Table 4.2 shows an application of this typology to identify stakeholders and their interests in the BRMP. The diversity of those identified in Table 4.2 is typical of such situations. Often there are numerous stakeholders at different levels who may be important to the decision-makers, or who are influential over the outcome of the decision. Stakeholders change over time; stakeholder interests and influence identified in one time period must be reconsidered rather than being immediately identified as relevant in the following time period. Stakeholder influence may be latent: land developers around BRMP, often absent from the island, retain development rights for years under the national planning system. Only when land changes hands do conflicts arise and their legitimacy is questioned. An ongoing, evolving map of interests and influences is an important first step in inclusive management.

Categorizing stakeholders into priority groups

In the first cut of a stakeholder analysis there is likely to be a long list of possible stakeholders demanding attention or requiring consideration. Categorizing stakeholders ensures that attention can be given to including and engaging the most important of these. This list needs to be prioritized to identify those who will be engaged actively in the coastal zone management process, those who will be consulted and those who will be kept informed of actions or events. In other words, stakeholders need to be categorized according to those whose claims and demands have the attention of decision-makers.

BOX 4.1 THE BUCCOO REEF MARINE PARK IN SOUTH-WEST TOBAGO

Buccoo Reef Marine Park (BRMP) is located in south-west Tobago in the eastern Caribbean and consists of the Buccoo Reef and the Bon Accord Lagoon Complex. The protected area encompasses a reef system that protects an extensive shallow lagoon bordered by a fringing mangrove wetland. It covers an area of 150ha plus a terrestrial area of 300ha (see Figure 4.2). The economy of Tobago is dependent on tourism and fishing. A key issue in the maintenance of livelihoods is the growing evidence that Tobago is a peripheral economy (the so-called 'second island' problem) in terms of the development of the service sectors in Trinidad and Tobago (Weaver, 1998). With an area of only 62km^2, the management of the coastal margins is critical to the whole island ecosystem.

The Buccoo Reef is one of the most visited recreational sites in Tobago. Both international and local visitors enjoy the beauty of the coral reefs, the clear waters and the abundant marine life that can be found there. Tourism has become an important contributor to local incomes yet it degrades the natural resource base on which many islanders directly depend for their livelihoods. Thus tourism brings benefits to Tobago, but not for everyone. The challenge is therefore to find ways of managing the Buccoo Reef that are acceptable to stakeholders while maintaining environmental quality to certain minimum standards.

The issue of how best to manage Buccoo Reef has been ongoing since the 1960s, when the appropriateness of clearing mangroves in the coastal zone to make way for tourism developments was questioned. The impacts of tourism development have been a major coastal zone management issue for Buccoo Reef ever since then.

Source: Based on Brown and others (2001b)

Stakeholder analysis originates from management science, where stakeholders are generally identified as those with stakes in public and private sector enterprises (see, for example, Mitchell and others, 1997). Mitchell and others suggest that the degree to which priority (a concept referred to as 'salience') should be given to stakeholders depends on the degree to which stakeholders possess each of the following three attributes:

1   *Power* (the stakeholders' ability to influence the decision made).
2   *Legitimacy* (the degree to which the stakeholders' relationships with the decision-maker have been established).
3   *Urgency* (the degree to which the stakeholders' needs require speedy action).

In essence, we can simplify this method by categorizing the stakeholders according to their level of influence and their importance to the decision-makers. Importance refers to the degree to which the stakeholder is considered a focus of the decision to be made. If the decision-makers are implementing a coastal zone management project designed solely to improve the livelihoods of the poor, for example, the poor who use the coast directly and indirectly would be the most important stakeholders. If, on the other hand, a coastal zone management project is developed primarily to conserve coastal ecosystems, then

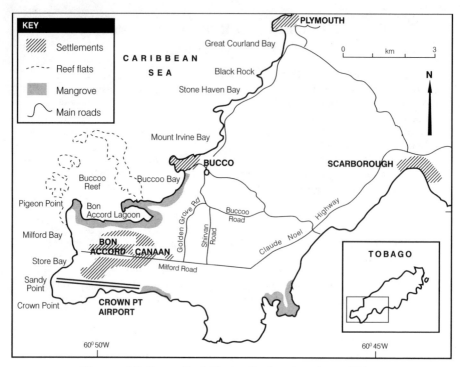

Figure 4.2 *Buccoo Reef Marine Park and south-west Tobago*

resource managers, resource owners and conservation agencies would be the most important stakeholders. Importance varies according to the objectives of the decision-makers.

Influence refers to the level of power a stakeholder has over the outcome of a decision. Influence is dictated by the stakeholders' control of, or access to, power and resources. Influential stakeholders, such as well-established lobbying groups, wealthy land-owners or respected religious leaders, often are already engaged in the decision-making process because they have access to it. Influence is not the same as importance. For example, a government ministry of finance is clearly highly influential in alleviating poverty, but it is the poor themselves who are the most important stakeholder group. Importance is usually determined by the policy-makers. Influence can be determined by the stakeholders themselves, or through independent reports on the stakeholder groups' access to power and resources.

Using this approach, the relative levels of influence and importance determine whether a stakeholder is primary, secondary or external. *Primary stakeholders* have little influence over the outcome of management decisions, but their welfare is important to the decision-makers. Often, the primary stakeholders are those who stand to lose the most from a decision, although this is not always the case. *Secondary stakeholders* can influence decisions because they are predominantly decision-makers and those engaged in implementing decisions. They are relatively unimportant as their welfare is not a priority, but it is important

Table 4.2 *Coastal stakeholders and their interests in the Buccoo Reef in Tobago*

Continuum level	Stakeholder groups	Interest in Buccoo Reef
Global and international society	European Union	Funding infrastructure development
	World Bank	Tying loans to compliance with international treaties
National	Town & Country Planning	Granting planning permissions
	Ministry of Finance	Funding government expenditure and projects
	Ministry of Tourism	Developing coastal tourism
	Ministry of Marine Resources and Fisheries	Developing coastal zone management strategies
Regional	Tobago House of Assembly	Planning and decision-making
	Water & Sewage Authority	Water and sewage treatment
	National Housing Authority	Managing housing estates
Local off-site	Buccoo villagers	Residents adjacent to BRMP
	Bon Accord/Mt Pleasant villagers	Residents inputting waste indirectly
	Mt Pleasant Credit Union	Managing sewage plant for Bon Accord/Canaan
	Hoteliers/restaurateurs	Waste run-off into the sea
	Taxi drivers	Taking tourists to Buccoo Reef
	Informal vendors	Selling marine shells to tourists
	Local land-owners not resident on their land	Valuable land for sale to hotel developers or other developers
Local on-site	Reef tour operators	Taking tourists to Buccoo Reef
	Reef patrol (local government)	Monitoring activity in BRMP
	Illegal fishers	Fishing within BRMP
	Illegal souvenir collectors	Extraction of shells from BRMP
	Legal fishermen	Access to fish-landing site
	Water-sports operators	Water-skiing/jet-skiing
	Tourists	Enjoying their visit to BRMP

Source: Brown and others (1999)

to remember that these groups are stakeholders. *External stakeholders* are those individuals or groups who can exert significant influence over the outcome of a process through lobbying the decision-makers, but whose interests are not important: church groups or NGOs might fall into this category.

Figure 4.3 shows the classification of the stakeholders for the BRMP according to their importance and influence. Plotting the stakeholders on these two axes enables an identification of the primary, secondary and external stakeholders. Clearly, groups such as local informal businesses and tour operators are dependent on the integrity of the resource system for their livelihoods. They stand to benefit from the conservation of the reefs and have direct interests. In Figure 4.3 they are shown to be high on the importance axis. But they have often been excluded from decision-making structures and hence lie low on the influence axis. Regulatory authorities and park managers have a lot of direct

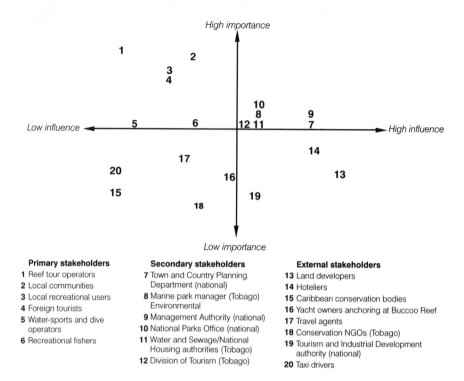

Figure 4.3 *Assessment of relative importance and influence of stakeholders in Buccoo Reef Marine Park*

influence on conservation outcomes but, as custodians of the ecosystems rather than dependents, they lie relatively low on the importance axis.

Other characteristics and dimensions of the relationships between stakeholders can be emphasized. Mikalsen and Jentoft (2001) assessed stakeholders according to the power–legitimacy–urgency typology for the Norwegian fishery (see Table 4.3). Instead of using these criteria to identify and classify primary, secondary and external stakeholders, Mikalsen and Jentoft describe three different sets of stakeholders, namely: definitive, expectant and latent stakeholders. *Definitive stakeholders* are those who possess all three qualities of power, legitimacy and urgency, so that they have an unequivocal claim on the attention of management. In management science, the manager of a firm must attend to the needs of such groups in order for the firm to survive. In the area of coastal zone management, the decision-makers must pay attention to the needs of these individuals or they may create political problems for the decision-makers.

Expectant stakeholders possess combinations of two out of the three attributes. They include those who are powerful and whose needs are urgent but have less legitimacy in current decision structures. The actions of these stakeholders can bring about flips in the institutional state. In the coastal context, an example would be an environmental lobby that has grown rapidly in membership following growth in public awareness about a specific issue. In 1995, the

Table 4.3 *Fisheries management stakeholders in Norway*

Stakeholders	Urgency	Power	Legitimacy
Definitive			
Fishers	High	High	High
Fish-processors	High	High	High
Bureaucrats	High	High	High
Enforcement agencies	High	High	High
Scientists	High	Medium	High
Fish workers	High	Medium	High
Expectant			
Indigenous peoples	High	Increasing	High
Environmental groups	Increasing	Increasing	Increasing
Local communities	Medium	Low	High
Latent			
Citizens	Increasing	Low	Increasing
The media	Increasing	Increasing	Low
Municipal authorities	Increasing	Medium	Increasing
Future generations	Low	Low	High
Banks	Low	High	Low
Consumers	Low	Low	Increasing
Equipment suppliers	Low	High	Medium
Tourist industries	Low	Medium	Low
Sports fishers	Low	Low	Increasing

Source: Mikalsen and Jentoft (2001)

Greenpeace campaign against the deep-sea dumping of the Brent Spar oil platform by Shell led to rapid growth in support for its stance that the oil platform should be disposed of on land. This campaign contributed to a change in the actual disposal strategy used by the company. Thus it demonstrated that expectant stakeholder groups can shift their legitimacy and use their powerful positions in radical ways, disturbing the management status quo.

Expectant stakeholders are also those who are legitimate and powerful, like employees and government agencies, but expect attention and usually already have some form of access to formal channels of communication. But equally, many stakeholders may have legitimate, urgent claims, but no power. These stakeholders will have to rely on advocacy and building alliances. Finally, *latent stakeholders* possess only one of the three attributes, and include powerful groups who have no motivation to use their power in the decision-making process, legitimate groups without power or any demand for urgent action, and groups with urgent needs that have no power and legitimacy. In whatever typology is appropriate for the coastal management situation, stakeholder analysis can highlight dynamism and the potential for all groups to move from one category to another by iterating the analysis over time.

Both of the typologies shown in Figure 4.3 and Table 4.3 offer useful mechanisms with which to consider the range of stakeholders. Both, however, require normative analysis of influence, importance, power, urgency and legitimacy. One stakeholder group may perceive the reality of the situation very differently to another. Hence stakeholder analysis in its current form remains a subjective expression of the possible roles of the different stakeholders on the decision-making stage.

Exploring stakeholder conflicts

Understanding who the stakeholders are and what their interests are enables an exploration of stakeholder conflicts. Conflict theory suggests that identifying conflicts of interest is the initial step in the conflict management process (Rijsberman, 1999). A pre-intervention conflict assessment of stakeholder interests can reveal perceived or actual conflicts among the stakeholders. For coastal resources, many stakeholder groups' interests are linked to their perceived and actual property and use rights. A lack of enforcement of legal property rights can lead to customary usage by stakeholders with no legal rights.

As demonstrated in the sets of stakeholders in the previous examples, stakeholder groups use coastal resources to support their livelihoods directly or indirectly. Increased demand for coastal zone or coastal resource use raises the possibility of conflict. This can manifest itself as direct use conflicts between the users, or indirect conflicts between the different objectives for the resource. In Northumberland in north-east England, a well documented case concerning the use of jet-skis illustrates these conflicts (Roe and Benson, 2001). No compromise could be reached.

Conflicts can clearly exist between on-site uses for the same resources. However, they can also exist at many scales on a continuum from the micro to the macro, as already highlighted in Chapter 3. Macro-scale issues relate to national, regional or international concerns, and micro-scale issues pertain to those concerns directly affecting the stakeholders at the local interface with the resource. Conflict can potentially exist between and across stakeholder groups at the different scales, and between the interests of international conventions and those of resource users (macro–micro), as well as between fishing and tourism, land development and local beach access, and a host of other macro–micro conflicts.

Who to include and who to exclude from deliberation

Having categorized the stakeholders, a rule of thumb is that the primary or definitive stakeholders should be included in the process, the secondary or expectant stakeholders should be consulted, and the external or latent stakeholders should be kept informed. This may appear to be a straightforward process. This would be true if all stakeholders were clearly identifiable and fell into specific groups. However, when individuals are not clearly distinguishable as members of one clearly defined group, such as the poor or the landless, it is difficult to categorize them.

In such situations, groups that contain target individuals (as defined by the management objectives) should be included in the primary stakeholder category even though they may not be categorized as such in the classification exercise. An example of this is migrants who have established themselves and are living on beachfront land, and who own their own dwellings. On first impressions it may appear that these stakeholders should be grouped with land-owners or sitting tenants as external stakeholders. However, such urban dwellers are often classified as 'squatters' and are unlikely to have access to resources and power, and hence are not in the same position as land-owners. Careful consideration of the range of members of stakeholder groups, and their access to power and resources, is necessary to avoid the misclassification of stakeholders and hence the exclusion of important groups.

Self-exclusion by stakeholders may occur. Groups who perceive that they may lose out, rightly or wrongly, from changes in a coastal management strategy may not feel inclined to engage in participatory processes at all. If a primary stakeholder group is reluctant to engage, the decision-maker may need to exhibit perseverance and some creativity to keep that group interested, engaged and participating in the process. Even if a primary stakeholder group will not engage immediately, participatory processes should be open enough to facilitate their joining the process when it becomes in their interests to do so. It has been suggested, for example, by Few (2001), that the compulsory engagement of stakeholders may in fact be a means of containing the actions of those stakeholders who operate outside the formal institutional structure. Few contends that stakeholders who desire to be excluded from a decision-making process should be entitled to remain on the outside if they feel that their ability to influence decision-making may be compromised by their inclusion.

There is also the possibility of self-selection by external or latent groups wishing to influence the deliberation process. Groups who are likely to benefit from biasing the decision-making process are likely to request to be included. The process has to ensure that their inclusion will not jeopardize the critical confidence-building process that is important in generating an active, deliberative process for the primary or definitive stakeholders.

In stakeholder processes it is difficult to ensure that there is an appropriate balance of stakeholders and that the appropriate level of involvement takes place. The most important thing is to constantly seek feedback from stakeholder participants in the decision-making process. Once together as a group, the primary stakeholders themselves can decide who is invited to engage in the process. The secondary stakeholders, who often include the managers of the resource, and the decision-makers should be included throughout the process, but they should not be allowed to dominate combined stakeholder group meetings. In those meetings, primary and secondary stakeholders must be treated equally and given equal time to talk. Managing the secondary stakeholders in the combined stakeholder meetings requires careful diplomacy.

At the outset of an inclusive, deliberative process, external or latent stakeholders should not be included despite the fact that they often wish to opt in for their own reasons. External stakeholders may be more vocal and more powerful, and are often perceived as having more status than the primary stakeholders, who may be intimidated by their presence. Their presence may inhibit both discussion and the open statement of preferences by other stakeholders. This can jeopardize the possibility of all the stakeholders working together at a later stage. External stakeholders should be informed of the ongoing process and kept up-to-date with actions and events.

Engagement techniques

A range of engagement techniques is available to bring stakeholders into a deliberative process. Engagement options depend on the nature of the group (see Table 4.4) and the most appropriate forum for them. Where organizations already exist and where the stakeholders are well known to each other and meet regularly, it is possible to hold focus groups in which certain issues can be discussed in carefully moderated meetings. However, with certain groups, particularly government agencies, where hierarchies exist and power balances are delicate, it may be necessary to engage the managers seperately so that they do not have to share their opinions with other staff. Not all groups have cohesive organizational structures with obvious points of contact and key spokespeople. If a group does exist, however loosely, it should be brought together in a focus group or another collective meeting, as these provide the most carefully managed environments in which to elicit information and build trust.

Some stakeholders are linked informally but do not belong to any organization or group. In this case, it is often very difficult to find a contact person, and all the stakeholders in these groups may need to be approached individually and invited to attend meetings to discuss the management issues. This can be a time-consuming process, but it ensures that those who are most disenfranchised and voiceless are given the opportunity to participate. There will be individuals who feel that, because they are illiterate or innumerate, they are not able to participate. These individuals should be encouraged to participate along with the others. All participants must be treated with equal respect, irrespective of their education, qualifications or ability to articulate their preferences and experience in the lexicon of management science.

If a group is unwilling to meet together at the outset, possibly because of conflicts within it, there are alternative methods of eliciting its opinions, such as individual interviews. Other coastal stakeholders, such as tourists, are unlikely to want to attend a meeting on their holiday. For these time-limited stakeholders, a questionnaire-type study is the most effective way of ensuring their participation in the process.

Working with stakeholders requires some consideration of the social and cultural settings within which the stakeholders operate to ensure that they are engaged in a socially and culturally appropriate manner. In general, there are some basic considerations that should be applied. All stakeholder group engagements should take place:

*   at a date, time and location suitable to the group;
*   with 4–10 people from the same stakeholder group; and
*   with some refreshments if the meeting lasts more than one hour.

Table 4.4 *Methods for engaging different types of stakeholder groups*

Techniques	Stakeholder groups	Characteristics of groups
Focus groups	Resident groups, fishers, tourist business operators, tour operators	Readily identifiable groups with formal but loose structures and stable membership
One-to-one structured and semi-structured interviews	Government officials, hoteliers	Individuals from hierarchical organization, often with widely different status within the organization. Tend to be reticent about freely expressing opinions in public or with peers
Informal questionnaire surveys	Non-formalized trade groups, eg street vendors	Transient, often on the margins of legality; reluctant to voice opinion in front of peers
Questionnaire	Recreational users	Transient and diverse

The time, date and location are important issues, and careful consideration should be given to them.

Stakeholders are not obliged to participate in participatory processes. Inviting a stakeholder to participate does not mean that he or she will. Stakeholders may have become fatigued with participatory research projects, they may simply have no faith in the participatory process or they may not prioritize participation. Trust has to be built in the decision-making process. If this can be achieved there is likely to be greater support for the decision made. The process must be open and honest about its objectives and the outcomes that stakeholders can realistically expect from their participation. Without honesty and openness stakeholders may exclude themselves deliberately, as demonstrated by the case of tour operators in the Buccoo Reef area who perceived that they were blamed for the past degradation of coral reefs in the area (see Box 4.2).

A wide range of methods can be used to engage stakeholders. Useful ways to make contact with stakeholders include public presentations and open meetings. Introducing a novel decision-making process in this way can be time-consuming. The benefit is that those most disenfranchised and voiceless may be reached and hence given the opportunity to participate. As a process of engagement progresses can be instigated. But trust requires action on both sides, and those investigating the decision problem must be willing to share information and expertise (see Box 4.3).

Understanding stakeholders' preferences

Knowing who the stakeholders are and how to engage them is a necessary part of decision support, but it is only a start. Including stakeholders in decision-making processes involves understanding different stakeholders' preferences, as these influence stakeholder behaviour and priority setting. Integrative approaches require participatory dialogues to enable stakeholders to deliberate

---

BOX 4.2 THE SELF-EXCLUSION OF THE BUCCOO REEF
TOUR OPERATORS

A video of the coral reef destruction at Buccoo Reef made by a local non-governmental organization (NGO) suggested that the main cause was the actions of reef tour operators who take tourists to walk on the reef in rubber boots. The video was shown throughout Trinidad and Tobago. As a result the news media condemned the reef tour operators for destroying the reef. The operators were not given the opportunity to put forward their case, which was that they affected only a tiny part of the reef by their activity, and that other factors (most notably run-off from the land) appeared to be causing more serious problems at Buccoo.

As a result of the video, the reef tour operators felt that they were being characterized as villains by conservationists, NGOs and government. When a participatory process was initiated in 1998 the facilitators invited the reef tour operators to the meetings. They were initially reluctant to come along to multi-group meetings as they felt that they would be criticized (in their opinion, unfairly) for their actions. As the reef tour operators are clearly primary stakeholders, central to the management decisions regarding BRMP, the invitation was repeated and kept open. The first meeting with the group was arranged through the Buccoo Reef Tour Operators' Cooperative. Gradually, through continual invitations to single stakeholder group meetings and by building trust, they became more involved in the process.

---

and discuss resource management issues in order to develop or refine their preferences. Including stakeholders' preferences in public decision-making about environmental goods and services requires some consideration of the nature of individuals' preferences and values. The importance of understanding individuals' preferences is clearly recognized in most of the social sciences (Baron, 1997). Resource allocation decisions have to be made that trade-off the benefits and costs of different environmental management strategies. Hence, as outlined in Chapter 3, there needs to be some understanding of how much people prefer one environmental management strategy to another when both strategies are demanded, such as conservation and development.

Recent sociology, philosophy and social psychology research emphasizes that people's preferences are socially constructed (see, for example, Sagoff, 1998; Gregory and Keeney, 1994; Beierle and Konisky, 2000). Consideration of a few concepts suggests that this is the case. For example, what is an 'acquired taste' if not a constructed preference that is generated as a result of trying something repeatedly and developing a modified opinion towards it with each attempt? In addition, how does a preference suddenly exist for a new good or service that has just been invented and introduced onto the market? In such a situation, an individual's preference might evolve through absorbing advertising information and through discussions with friends or acquaintances who have used the product. Finally, there is much research on preference reversal in the field of environmental economics valuation that suggests that people's preferences are not fixed, but are context- and information-dependent (see, for example, Gregory and Slovic, 1997).

BOX 4.3 BUILDING TRUST WITH THE PEOPLE OF BUCCOO

To initiate trust in the participatory process, the facilitators first made a presentation on water quality and the impact of tourism on Buccoo Reef in 1998. Water quality was a controversial issue at the time. It had been in the local newspapers in the weeks before the presentation. The team was aware of the difficulty that local residents experienced in obtaining information, and thought that stakeholders who had provided information to other researcher groups might be interested in the results of previous research, particularly research that was not easily accessible in public records.

Formal letters of invitation were sent to stakeholders for whom the team had contact addresses, including government agencies. The invitations described the research team and the participatory project and invited the individual and their stakeholder group to attend the meeting. Public announcements were made on the local radio station, and invitations were handed out at the central market on a Saturday morning and in the local villages adjacent to Buccoo Reef.

The meeting was scheduled for a night that did not clash with either government community meetings or village council meetings. It was held in the evening to enable maximum attendance. It was chaired by the manager of the marine park and was supported by various government officials. All these factors contributed to a high turnout on the night. One-page presentation summaries, including contact information, were distributed. Interested parties were encouraged to ask directly for more information at the presentation. A broad selection of stakeholders attended. Those present were asked if they would like to be invited to similar meetings, or to engage in further discussions about Buccoo Reef. They were also asked to inform the speakers of any other people who would be interested in such events or in the management of Buccoo Reef.

Individual preferences for environmental goods and services are dynamic and evolving, and are dependent as much on the perception of environmental change and culture as on their relative 'scarcity'. Norton and others (1998) discuss arguments for and against the assumption of fixed or flexible preferences in economic analysis. If it is assumed that individuals' preferences are clearly formed and fixed, then the researcher merely needs to ask the respondent to elucidate their preference, such as through a 'willingness to pay' question concerning environmental change. If, on the other hand, preferences are actually socially constructed and individuals learn about goods and services through information and discussion, and through this learning process develop their preferences, then deliberation is an important part of the value elicitation process (Norton and others, 1998).

The role of information in decision-making

Identifying, characterizing and then engaging stakeholders are the first steps towards participatory conservation and development in the coastal zone. Engagement does not in itself generate supported decisions. Rational decision-making processes involve weighing up the advantages and disadvantages of any management options and assessing how the net benefits can be maximized.

Information is needed to undertake such a weighing-up process, and to answer the questions that the stakeholders may have about resource management alternatives. Such information may include scientific information about coastal systems and the distribution of economic costs and benefits, as well as stakeholder knowledge about the local resources and their management preferences. A transparent and comprehensible framework in which this information can be displayed, compared and analysed is necessary to give meaning to bigger-picture questions.

But, as well as understanding stakeholders' preferences for different management options, decision-makers have to understand the impacts of the different decisions. Without information to describe the potential impacts of the different management goals described in the alternative future development scenarios, decision-makers may find it very difficult to make a fully informed decision about multiple-use resources. As Petry (1990) notes, 'the simple fact of showing the decision-makers the double-entry table of their expected consequences on all criteria, with comments on their significance and essential features ... might be sufficient as a basis for decision' (Petry, 1990, p220).

The trade-off analysis framework outlined below and elucidated in Chapter 5 specifically enables the inclusion of stakeholders' preferences at many different stages of the decision-making process, thus ensuring that stakeholders' perceptions and preferences are expressed, considered and incorporated. As a caveat to this, while decision-support tools may contribute to the rationality of the decision-making process, they do not necessarily improve the quality of the decision made (Steins and Edwards, 1999) in terms of distribution equity, efficiency and effectiveness in meeting stated objectives. But institutional change cannot be sustainable without the legitimacy and trust that stakeholders engender.

In the following section we present a suite of techniques that have been developed and applied in what we have termed 'trade-off analysis'. The rest of this chapter introduces some of the initial stages in such an analysis. The next chapter examines in detail the assessment and evaluation of different development options, and the definition and measurement of criteria with which to evaluate these options using a multi-criteria analysis (MCA) within the trade-off analysis framework. Using this method in a participatory way to facilitate deliberation with a range of stakeholder groups distinguishes our approach from conventional decision analysis. In Chapter 6 the implications of these techniques for inclusionary processes and building trust and consensus are discussed.

TRADE-OFF ANALYSIS

Trade-off analysis supports decisions for coastal zone management by explicitly including all relevant stakeholders in a deliberative process to assess alternative management strategies. Different forms of knowledge and information are structured, organized and analysed, but decisions are reached by a number of different consensus-building and conflict-resolution techniques. This approach thereby deals directly with the challenges set out in this chapter and supports inclusionary, multiple-stakeholder and co-management approaches to coastal resource management.

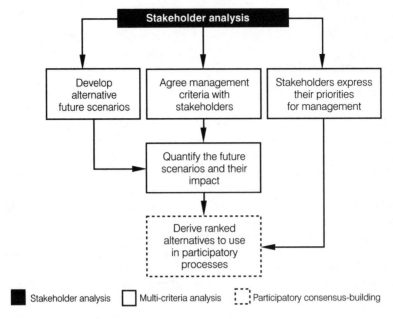

Figure 4.4 *Stages in the trade-off analysis process*

Towards a framework

The trade-off analysis approach initially uses stakeholder analysis to inform the design of the economic, social and ecological evaluation of options, and to identify who should be involved in the deliberative processes for enhanced management. The strategy then uses MCA to organize information and facilitate evaluation of the options and their impacts. The social, economic and ecological evaluation of the impacts of options is generated using primary and secondary data. The scenarios and information derived from this exercise are used to increase the level of engagement with the stakeholder groups. The subsequent stakeholder participatory process defines and refines the objectives of management. Figure 4.4 summarizes the techniques and steps involved in this trade-off analysis approach.

The process of stakeholder involvement outlined in this chapter makes explicit the different perceptions and values of the different actors, which creates opportunities for decision-making and management based on consensus rather than conflict. The trade-offs are quantified, where relevant, with reference to the techniques of environmental economics, social analysis and ecological modelling. The involvement of stakeholders in the process of developing the model, and in discussing the recommendations derived from different weightings, provides an opportunity to explore and construct different development outcomes or scenarios.

The trade-off analysis framework recognizes the importance of stakeholder, manager and researcher learning in the decision-making process and the evolution of preferences over time. The framework is flexible and enables interaction between the three system components of stakeholder analysis, MCA and consensus-building techniques (Figure 4.4) throughout the process.

Multi-criteria analysis

Techniques of MCA are adopted as part of trade-off analysis because of their flexibility in handling complex information, and because of the need in trade-off analysis to be sensitive to the construction of values within priority-setting. MCA usually proceeds by generating information about the decision problem from available data and ideas, effectively generating solutions (alternatives) and providing a transparent understanding of the structure and content of the decision problem.

There are range of MCA models that manipulate and analyse information. The choice of an appropriate MCA model is determined by the objectives of the decision-maker. If the decision-maker is seeking to explore a range of scenarios from which to make a selection, a multi-objective decision model (MODM) may be most appropriate. Alternatively, if the decision-maker wants to make a choice from a finite number of scenarios a multi-attribute decision model (MADM) is more appropriate.

MCA has a long history of explaining, rationalizing or predicting decision-making behaviour (for example, Hwang and Yoon, 1981). Many disciplines, such as decision theory, economics, statistics and psychometrics, have contributed to the development of these methods (Kersten, 1997). Within the set of MCA options, there is little agreement about how to select the appropriate method to use (Guitouni and Martel, 1998). Most MCA users will select a method they are familiar with rather than the optimal method (objective- or attribute-based models).

One of the most important features in selecting an MCA tool for use with stakeholder groups is that the tool should not be cognitively complex for the decision-maker or the individual stakeholders (see Joubert and others, 1997). Transparency of the decision-making process is another important feature of any decision-support tool (Hobbs and others, 1992). Olson and others (2000) note that without transparency and simplicity, decision-support tools are not likely to be useful in practical situations. Variants of the MCA models have widely been applied to areas as diverse as salmon fishery recovery schemes in the USA, river basin planning in south India and coral reef management in the Caribbean (see, for example, Fernandes and others, 1999; Chesson and others, 1999; Gurocak and Whittlesey, 1998; Moriki and others, 1996; Raj, 1995). The trade-off analysis approach in the Buccoo Reef case study described here uses an MADM because of its simplicity in presenting information concerning prescribed scenarios and the choices between them.

MCA requires an identification of the possible development options and an assessment of the impacts of those options on a set of management criteria. MCA then ranks the development options in terms of their impacts on the criteria. Multiple users' preferences for different management priorities can be included through the use of weights. The weighted ranking of development options can be compared to inform decision-makers about the level of support for, and the possible impact of, their decisions.

Within trade-off analysis MCA is used to support a process by which diverse stakeholders can examine information on criteria and impacts and explore the outcomes and impacts of decisions made as a result of different priorities. This is promoted through each stakeholder group applying their own weights to the economic, social and ecological criteria. It is therefore process-oriented rather than outcome-orientated where the MCA is used as a tool to facilitate the deliberations of stakeholders. MCA offers opportunities to present the trade-offs and rank different priorities and criteria in a systematic manner that does not specify one overall value framework. It allows the sensitivity of both social and physical data to be tested, and makes explicit the trade-offs between competing impacts and stakeholders.

CONCLUSION

Long experience from research into applying MCA suggests that it is a valuable tool for achieving resolutions to environmental conflicts. However, there are several constraints in practice. Critical elements to enable participation in decision-making include the clear identification of the relevant interest groups, the interactions between the interest groups and the socio-economic activities undertaken by the interest groups. Following on from these lessons, participatory decision-making using MCA as the organizing framework is the only way to ensure legitimacy, trust and openness and to overcome suspicions that MCA is another planners' toy.

We developed trade-off analysis in the context of BRMP in Tobago. The application of trade-off analysis to the decision problem for Buccoo Reef – namely, how to balance conservation and development in a marine protected area – is described fully in Chapter 5. As we have shown here, the necessary first step is the identification of and engagement with appropriate stakeholders.

Chapter 5

Doing Trade-off Analysis

Coastal zone managers have to juggle dual objectives: the sustainable management of the complex ecological systems that coexist at the land–water interface, and the development needs of the stakeholders and institutions that operate in the social and economic settings within the coastal zone. Balancing these two objectives involves negotiating between conservation and development initiatives in the coastal zone and making trade-offs between coastal uses.

As noted in Chapter 4, trade-off analysis is one means of bridging the gap between the scientific management of ecosystems and development planning for society and the wider economy. The trade-off analysis approach is described in this chapter in detail using the Buccoo Reef Marine Park (BRMP) in Tobago as a case study. The trade-off analysis approach begins with an exploration of the stakeholders, as described in Chapter 4, and continues in this chapter with the creation of a multi-criteria analysis (MCA) model. This includes the development of alternative future scenarios and the selection of evaluation criteria with which to assess the impacts of these scenarios.

DESIGNING ALTERNATIVE FUTURE DEVELOPMENT SCENARIOS

Evaluating different management options is a key part of decision-making, as outlined in Chapter 4. To do this, we estimate the likely impacts of the different management approaches on the coastal zone and coastal stakeholders by envisioning how the future might look. The impacts will depend on many factors: for example, whether there are more or fewer coastal users, more or fewer pollutants entering the coastal environment and the level of environmental lobbying. Future scenarios reveal possible combinations of these factors. A scenario is simply a 'coherent, internally consistent and plausible description of a possible future state of the world' (Carter and La Rovere, 2001). Based on these driving factors it is possible to generate a range of scenarios that describe several broadly acceptable futures. Starting with coarsely-defined scenarios, the scenarios can be fine-tuned to reveal limits to the range of policies that need to be considered.

Scenario use is well established, and examples of scenarios and their use can be found in decision analysis and, increasingly, in the diverse areas of environmental change. In decision-support theory, Stewart and Scott (1995) suggest identifying as many policy elements and driving factors as possible through discussions with planners and decision-makers. These policy elements influence the future of the coastal zone even though they are not necessarily on the coast, and might include reservoir development, water and land use restrictions, investment in water supply and sewage-handling schemes. For each policy element a maximum and minimum change should then be considered: for example, land use planners cannot completely reverse existing land use patterns, but they can change their policy on future land uses. Scenarios can then be developed by considering combinations of the feasible options for each policy element. Stewart and Scott (1995) note that there are two main problems with this approach. First, the number of scenarios that can be created are infinite, yet there are limits to the cognitive processing skills of individuals and the time and resources available to estimate the impacts of the different scenarios. Thus a degree of subjective judgement has to be applied to limit the number of possible scenarios. Second, if there are many scenarios, a lot of time and effort may need to be spent on background research, data collection and modelling for each scenario.

There is a flourishing industry of research into future global and regional scenarios in the context of global environmental change. Some of this research develops storylines and describes futures for total human population, land use, energy use and a host of related physical and biological systems and feedbacks (for example, O'Neill and others, 2001; Carter and La Rovere, 2001). Much of this scenario development supports insights into climate change and its causes and consequences. Only occasionally are such scenarios developed in consultation with stakeholders, or their consequences explored in an interactive manner. One such example is the work of Lorenzoni and others (2000) investigating global climate change in a local setting. They explored issues concerning how stakeholders perceive scenarios in general. They demonstrated that the values and views on governance held by the individual stakeholders fundamentally altered the manner in which scenarios were interpreted. Some storylines of the future can be more believable, for example, if you have faith that technologies and progress will solve most of the world's problems.

Scenario analysis never takes place in a vacuum and needs to build on the way in which the future is already being planned. Where management plans or strategies for the coastal zone already exist, these are the best sources of information to enable the definition of alternative future development scenarios. These plans may have been generated by government, research institutes, developers or academics. In all countries, central and local governments undertake some levels of planning, whereby they make short-term, medium-term or roll-over financial plans and spatial development plans. Such development plans indicate the planned areas for economic growth, planned areas of expansion and areas in which government is willing to target spending.

Where development plans or very specific management plans have already been developed, a range of alternative scenarios still needs to be developed focusing on coastal management and the interests of competing stakeholders. National development plans can give a very clear idea of the type of development strategy a country is following. However, this information has to be read and understood in the light of actual actions that the government is taking. For example, if a government places a moratorium on new hotel developments and then gives planning permission for a new hotel, the spatial land use plans will lack credibility and legitimacy in the eyes of many.

The possibility of inaction, a 'do-nothing' scenario, also needs to be considered. It is often the case that no action is taken if a decision is considered politically difficult. Such inaction creates outcomes that need to be evaluated. The absence of a decision is a policy in itself. The art of 'non-decision-making' involves postponing decisions by kicking them into the long grass of inquiry or further assessment. It also involves making sure that controversial issues simply do not make it onto the agenda. For example, a lack of planned investments to improve sewage treatment in a country where there is no sewage treatment to higher water quality standards (such as tertiary level) might imply one of three things. That sewage treatment is not a problem. That it is a recognized problem but no funds can be found for investment. Or that it is a problem but it has effectively been kept off the agenda. In all cases, development scenarios should be understandable to the layperson, distinctly different from each other, possible and realistic, clear and transparent, and – if possible – substantiated by existing information. But scenarios also need to be cognisant of the political realities: why some futures seem more plausible than others, and the history of decision-making and non-decision-making.

Defining scenarios for Buccoo Reef

In the case of BRMP, the scenarios of future change are based on existing development plans and knowledge about the challenges facing Tobago. Desk research combined with discussions over several months with planners and other government stakeholders revealed that two issues were the most important driving forces that could affect Tobago's development in the short and medium term: the level of environmental management and the level of tourism development.

In the late 1990s the Tobago House of Assembly commissioned a 15-year development plan for Tobago. Various development actions were promoted within this plan, including an economic growth rate of 10–15 per cent per annum. The plan recommended that this growth be generated through tourism development. One scenario had therefore to reflect a very rapid increase in visitor expenditure in Tobago: it was assumed that this would come through increased arrivals. Another reflected what would happen if growth remained as it was. Thus the scenarios reflected futures with and without policy intervention.

Given the potential growth in the tourism sector and the related increase in the number of tourists, the level of waste produced could only rise. A range of waste management systems had been considered by Trinidad and Tobago's Water and Sewerage Authority. These systems included a central waste management system that would be very expensive initially but would represent a

Table 5.1 *Scenarios for Buccoo Reef Marine Park and the driving forces of change*

Scenario	New tourist beds in BRMP area	Population in BRMP area	Percentage tertiary treated waste
A: Limited tourism development without complementary environmental management	240	6900	10
B: Limited tourism development with complementary environmental management	240	6900	50
C: Expansive tourism development without complementary environmental management	1580	7400	20
D: Expansive tourism development with complementary environmental management	1580	7400	70

significant upgrade of the existing waste treatment facilities. The other options included developing regional waste treatment stations and leaving existing 'soakaway' systems in place. To ensure that all the possible options were reflected in the scenarios for the region, one reflected possible improvements in waste treatment and another reflected the absence of change.

Tourism development and environmental management were therefore the two driving forces of change that informed the shape of the alternative future development scenarios. Each driver was estimated according to 'no change' and 'realistic change', as defined by the environmental management plans and the development plans for economic growth. The values for these factors are displayed in Table 5.1.

The four scenarios are named A, B, C and D for the sake of neutrality of language (see O'Hara, 1996). They do not represent inevitable development outcomes that particular stakeholder groups and vested interests might oppose. An important aspect of the scenarios is that they represent feasible and believable futures for local stakeholders. The advantage of stakeholder involvement at this stage of the trade-off analysis approach is, therefore, that the scenarios are not perceived as being separate from the reality of development planning, but rather as credible descriptions of the options facing south-west Tobago.

CHOOSING BETWEEN ALTERNATIVE FUTURE SCENARIOS

Each alternative future coastal zone management scenario is likely to create differential impacts, both positive and negative, on different stakeholder groups. The impacts of scenarios in the context of coastal resources can generally be split into three groups: economic, socio-cultural and environmental. Depending on the local situation other impacts could be very important, such as access to

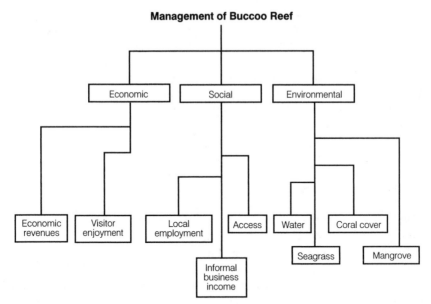

Figure 5.1 *A tree diagram of the decision problem for Buccoo Reef Marine Park*

resources, ownership rights and the impact of pollution, specifically on the elderly or children.

Management criteria that reflect the impacts of the alternative future scenarios are compiled through discussion with specialists and the stakeholders affected by the changes. As discussed in Chapter 4, there are various methods to engage with the stakeholders and elicit their preferences, depending on circumstances and the nature of the stakeholder. Tree diagrams can be used as an effective means of ensuring that a wide range of criteria are considered by stakeholders. A tree diagram uses stems and branches to conceptualize the range of possible impacts that result from a decision. At the apex of the tree, the main issue under consideration is stated: this is usually management-focused. On the branches leading from this node are the 'evaluation criteria'. These are general issues of concern, such as the economy, society and ecological health, although there could be many others. On the branches leading from these nodes are the more detailed and descriptive concerns, the 'measurable indicators'.

Figure 5.1 provides an example of the use of a tree diagram to identify the main issues of concern for the Buccoo Reef area. Here the main issue is developing sustainable management for the Buccoo Reef complex. The three evaluation criteria are economic growth, social issues and environmental health issues. These evaluation criteria can be measured by nine measurable indicators: macroeconomic benefits from tourism development, recreational users' enjoyment of Buccoo Reef, new full-time jobs for Tobagonians, livelihoods of informal business vendors, access for local residents to Buccoo Reef, water quality, the integrity of systems, coral reef quality in Buccoo Reef and the maintenance of mangroves.

All stakeholders need to be involved in the selection of evaluation criteria. Local residents may not be aware of the important and complex environmental impacts of certain developments. Conversely, regulators or scientists may not be aware of the specific local circumstances that are liable to be affected by management. The value tree may represent a large number of measurable indicators. To arrive at a representative and manageable set of indicators, the following five conditions can be tested.

1   **Is the list complete?** Do the criteria identified describe all the main issues of concern to the decision-maker and the primary stakeholders?
2   **Is the list operational?** Are all of the measurable indicators specific enough for the decision-maker to evaluate and compare the different scenarios? The measurable indicators do not necessarily need to describe the exact interaction of each system component. They need only reflect changes in the economic, social or ecological systems as a result of the alternative management decisions. The information is ultimately used by all stakeholders: too much detail can be as confusing as too little detail.
3   **Has double-counting occurred?** Can the performance of each evaluation criterion under the different development scenarios be judged independently from the other criteria?
4   **Do the criteria vary under the scenarios?** There is no point using criteria that do not vary across the scenarios, and gathering data to measure them wastes scarce resources.
5   **Has the list been kept to a minimum size?** Have the measurable indicators been kept to the smallest number to minimize the potential for confusion by the stakeholders when making trade-offs between criteria? In general, 8 to 15 measurable indicators are usually appropriate for most problems, although the fewer the better.

The measurable indicators can be further fine-tuned by applying the condition of measurability. Measurability refers to the ability to measure an indicator accurately. There is no hard and fast rule to determine this. If an indicator cannot be represented by a value, whether qualitative or quantitative, it is probably not useful.

Defining criteria for Buccoo

The evaluation criteria for the MCA in Buccoo were selected in a participatory manner. An initial comprehensive set of evaluation criteria were elicited from a review of conservation and development management decisions that had been made for the region. This draft set of criteria was circulated widely at open public meetings in south-west Tobago. At these meetings both the government and the non-governmental stakeholders expressed their preferences regarding the criteria by which decisions about the future of BRMP should be made.

The resulting set of economic, social and ecological criteria are related to the impacts of national and local economic growth and environmental management on community, social development and cultural integrity as well as

Table 5.2 *Criteria for assessing management options for Buccoo Reef Marine Park and method of estimation*

Criteria	Sub-criteria	Measure/basis of calculation
Economic criteria	1 Macroeconomic benefits of tourism to Trinidad and Tobago	Tourism revenue x economic multiplier x (1-marginal propensity to import)
	2 Tourist benefits	Consumer surplus of recreational users of BRMP
Social criteria	3 Local employment in tourism	Additional full-time 'quality' jobs x proportion of jobs to Tobagonians
	4 Informal sector benefits	Changes in informal sector benefits
	5 Costs of local access to BRMP	Change in costs of accessing BRMP for recreation and subsistence-extractive purposes
Ecological criteria	6 Water quality	Nutrient concentration, nitrate loading and concentration
	7 Productivity of seagrasses	Unit productivity
	8 Coral reef health	% live coral cover
	9 Mangrove habitat	Change in area of mangrove (ha)

on environmental conservation. The measurable indicators do not describe all the systems under consideration and are not therefore an attempt to develop a comprehensive ecosystem model (for example, Bockstael and others, 1995). Rather, the measurable indicators are usable and widely understood indicators of important aspects of the overall picture as perceived by the major stakeholder groups. The final selection of indicators depended on the indicators being measurable across the different scenarios. The development and estimation of the indicators were discussed with the stakeholders as the project progressed. Table 5.2 describes the criteria and the selected measurable indicators for the Buccoo Reef case, with a brief explanation of their measurement.

ASSESSING THE IMPACTS OF THE DIFFERENT DEVELOPMENT SCENARIOS ON THE CRITERIA

Operationalizing an MCA involves estimating the effects of the scenarios on each measurable indicator in quantitative or semi-quantitative form. The strategy for data collection involves diverse techniques across the ecological, social and economic criteria. Some of the techniques used to quantify each of the nine measurable indicators are now described in detail.

Economic criteria for Buccoo

The economic criteria for Buccoo focus on macroeconomic benefits and recreational user benefits. The first of these is the primary concern of economic planners who aim to maximize revenues to the public and private sector

(Economic measurable indicator 1). Recreational benefits to local and foreign recreational users (Economic measurable indicator 2) are important non-market benefits captured by that stakeholder group. Further, the second indicator is an indirect indicator of the sustainability of tourism based in part on the quality of the marine and coastal environment. The first indicator, macroeconomic benefits, is derived from total annual visitor expenditure in the relevant unit of assessment, namely south-west Tobago. This estimate of revenue is the gross benefit to the immediate region from tourism. The net figure is dependent on the rate of leakage from the economy, a critical issue for many small island and particularly second island states (see, for example, Weaver, 1998). Thus the net macroeconomic benefit is estimated using Tobago's marginal propensity to import and the 'tourism multiplier', which reflects the benefits that accrue across the economy from the initial round of tourist expenditure, thereby showing the macroeconomic benefits that accrue to south-west Tobago. The results are estimates of net present value ranging from US$9.1 million to $18.7 million across the scenarios. The indicators all refer to a ten-year time horizon from 1997 to 2007.

The second economic measurable indicator, tourist benefits, reflects visitor perceptions of the BRMP. The economic value of this benefit to tourists has been estimated as the total willingness to pay (WTP) of visitors to south-west Tobago, both users and non-users of the park, using a contingent valuation survey based on a random survey of 1000 visitors and residents. Consumers' surplus of recreation has been estimated for coastal and marine resources in a variety of contexts through revealed and expressed preference methods and other economic analyses (for example, Bell and Leeworthy, 1990; Berg and others, 1998; Ruitenbeek and Cartier, 2001a).

The contingent valuation survey at Buccoo Reef revealed how much those in the sample were willing to pay to prevent further deterioration in the quality of Buccoo Reef (ie, to prevent a loss). This type of question enables an estimation of equivalent surplus measures of welfare change. The contingent valuation study generated estimates of change in equivalent surplus over the four scenarios to 2007. The equivalent surplus generated from visitor and resident use of BRMP is estimated for both the existing level of environmental quality and other levels of environmental quality. There are other ways to frame such a study and other estimates of welfare change, such as the willingness to accept compensation for a loss. This framing always needs careful consideration: in this case the property rights are such that WTP is most appropriate (see discussion in Brown and others, 2001b).

The mean WTP across all respondents, including those not willing to pay, ranged from US$3.70 to $9.30. The range of mean values reflects different methods in the survey. The lower figure comes from an open-ended survey in which the respondents were asked, in essence, 'how much would you be willing to pay?'; the upper end of the range comes from dichotomous choice questions, in which the respondents were asked to reply 'yes' or 'no' to the question: 'would you be willing to pay $X?'. The amounts specified (X) varied between respondents. There is no correct answer in designing these surveys, and there is

Table 5.3 *Estimated total willingness to pay for recreational use of Buccoo Reef Marine Park under different development scenarios*

	BRMP quality reduced (Scenario A)	No change (Scenario B)	BRMP quality reduced + double number of users (Scenario C)	Double number of users (Scenario D)
NPV of WTP to maintain or prevent deterioration (US$m)	2.5	2.5	3.7	3.7
Percentage of those willing to pay who would still pay under new scenario	49%	100%	23%	46%
NPV of total WTP to 2007 (US$m)	1.2	2.5	0.9	1.7

Note: NPV = net rpesent value.

a huge and ongoing debate as to the interpretation of results of such surveys for use in environmental decision-making. Open-ended survey design, for example, is recognized to give lower-bound estimates because of free-rider effects. Some respondents tend to give lower estimates because they perceive that others will bid more and the environment will be conserved anyway. Summaries of these and other arguments are dealt with in detail in Bateman and Willis (1999).

In the case of the Buccoo Reef survey, respondents were asked if they would still be willing to pay under different scenarios of changes in the level of tourism development and environmental management. This enabled the researchers to determine the effects of different scenarios on WTP. Under the 'without environmental management' scenarios it is assumed that water quality will decline. This would reduce the expected sightings of fish and coral through coral death and poorer water visibility. Respondents indicated that if average water visibility were halved, 49 per cent would still be willing to pay. If the number of people at the site doubled, 46 per cent would still be willing to pay. If the average visibility was halved and the number of visitors at the site doubled, 23 per cent of respondents would still be willing to pay.

Table 5.3 shows that the potential revenue is maximized over the ten-year timeframe under the scenarios of expansive tourism development, because this maximizes the number of visitors to the site in the short term. The results in Table 5.3 do not, however, reflect the longer-term environmental, and subsequent economic, impacts of high levels of direct use of BRMP. The resulting estimates show an equivalent surplus of between US$0.6 million and $2.5 million in net present value (NPV), depending on the resulting environmental quality implied by the scenarios.

Social criteria for Buccoo

The social criteria, the third, fourth and fifth measurable indicators in Table 5.2, reflect the distribution and social impact of the development scenarios. Developed in consultation with stakeholder groups, they include local employment, the contribution of the informal sector to local livelihoods and local access to BRMP. As outlined in Chapter 1, tourism creates many social problems and challenges, from increased crime rates to changes in cultural values and health and other factors (see Pattullo, 1996 on the Caribbean, for example). The social criteria developed here, however, reflect the overwhelming focus of the stakeholder groups on employment and social factors that they feel are often excluded from decision-making based on economic analysis. The qualitative and quantitative measurable indicators have been estimated using the methods and data outlined in Table 5.2.

Local employment in tourism reflects the ability of the Tobago tourism sector to reduce Tobagonian unemployment. More specifically, this measurable indicator incorporates the absolute level of employment as well as unemployment among Tobagonians, as indicated by the absolute number of full-time equivalent direct and indirect jobs for Tobagonians. This measurable indicator reflects local concern about the apparently high leakage rate of employment from Tobago, as well as the differentials in skilled employment rates between Trinidad and Tobago (Coppin and Olsen, 1998). Only those jobs in the tourism sector (including wholesale and retail outlets) which pay Tobagonians the estimated poverty line wage (US$160 per month in 1997) or above were included. Fifty-four per cent of wage earners in the tourism sector were reported to earn above this level in a 1996 labour force survey. There are approximately 2.3 direct tourism jobs per tourist accommodation room. For Tobagonians this potentially translates into 1.2 direct, above-minimum-wage jobs created per room, as well as 1.7 indirect jobs per room created through the construction of accommodation. Multiplying these estimates of employment creation opportunities by scenarios of tourism development to 2007 results in estimates for the numbers of new quality direct and indirect jobs. These estimates represent jobs that are likely to be created under the expansive and limited tourism development scenarios.

The purpose of the informal sector indicator is to estimate the impacts of changes in environmental management and tourism development on the small traders who fall outside the formal tourism sector but whose activities are an important source of livelihoods for Tobagonians. Little research has been undertaken to assess the level of trade generated by informal tourism vendors, perhaps due to the problems of data collection and the potential problems of interviewing vendors about their business activity (Harriss, 1992). This indicator was estimated across the scenarios by eliciting the perceptions of those involved in the informal tourism sector to derive qualitative scores for the impacts of scenarios on their livelihoods.

A face-to-face survey was carried out to elicit the perceptions of a sample of 30 informal business vendors. The sample represented approximately 70 per

Table 5.4 *Impacts of scenarios for Buccoo Reef on livelihoods of informal business vendors*

Scenario drivers	With enhanced environmental management	Impact on livelihoods of informal business vendors	Without enhanced environmental management	Impact on livelihoods of informal business vendors
Expansive tourism development	Larger hotels (own craft shops)	1	Larger hotels (own craft shops)	1
	Increased management may lead to removal of vendors	1	No change in environmental or park management	2
Limited tourism development	Smaller hotels (more adventurous tourists)	3	Smaller hotels (more adventurous tourists)	3
	Increased management may lead to removal of vendors	1	No change in environmental or park management	2

Notes: 1 represents negative impact; 2 represents no significant impact; 3 represents positive impact (see text)
Source: Generated from qualitative responses to survey of informal businesses (see text)

cent of all vendors in south-west Tobago. Respondents were asked about their perceptions of the structure of the informal sector, how additional tourists would affect their business, and how other changes to the tourism industry might affect their business. The survey found that 83 per cent of those interviewed rely on the informal sector for 50 per cent or more of their income, suggesting that while the sector itself is small it provides an important source of income for those involved. Respondents identified three main issues that affected their livelihoods. These were: the size and nature of the hotels to be developed, the kinds of tourists likely to visit Tobago (correlated with the kinds of hotels constructed), and the level of park and beach management. Table 5.4 describes the overall impacts on informal sector livelihoods of the three issues under the different scenarios.

If the majority of respondents felt that an impact could improve their livelihood, it scored three. If it was deemed to not have much impact it scored two, and if it was felt to have a negative impact it scored one. These scorings have ordinal properties, reflecting respondents' preference orderings of the impacts of the different scenarios. The scores in Table 5.4 have been derived from the qualitative analysis of the vendors' responses in the questionnaires. Some informal business vendors indicated that if there is expansive growth in the number of hotels in south-west Tobago there is likely to be a simultaneous rise in the number of hotel-run shops. It was perceived that this would reduce the level of demand for the goods provided by two-thirds of informal vendors. By contrast, some of the vendors believed that if growth in the number of hotels was restricted and only smaller hotels were allowed, the informal vendors would benefit from the increased number of tourists on the island, possibly leading to an increase in their sales. For each scenario, two scores were recorded revealing the respondents' relative preferences towards two issues: the level of tourism development and the level of environmental management. The two scores were added together to provide an ordinal ranking of the respondents' preferences for the different scenarios. Thus qualitative as well as quantitative data, ordinal as well as cardinal, can be used to paint a picture of future options and impacts.

Similarly, access by Tobagonians to the BRMP for recreation is an important factor identified by local residents (the fifth measurable indicator). An assessment of the locations and impacts of proposed beachside developments within the scenarios was undertaken and converted to scaled scores using the expert judgement of the regulating agency. Large-scale beachside tourism development has often restricted coastal access for local recreational users. The impact scores were included in the MCA using the same scaling device as for the informal sector (see above) and were converted to ordinal scores (see, for example, Bernard, 1994). It is important to note that not all indicators are represented in quantitative terms, and that social indicators, in particular, can utilize qualitative data in ways that are meaningful and understandable to stakeholder groups.

Ecological criteria for Buccoo

For coral reef systems in general, water quality is of paramount importance, and it represents one of the major indicators of ecosystem health. Water quality under the different scenarios for Buccoo Reef is indicated by the projected ambient concentrations of total nitrates in the marine environment in 2007. It has been estimated that approximately 80 per cent of all marine pollution in the Caribbean comes from land-based sources, primarily through run-off as a result of agriculture and land use change (Rawlins and others, 1998). The impacts of increased sediment loading and nutrient loading and the presence of other pollutants on coral reefs and related systems is relatively well researched. In general, coral reef systems thrive in low-nutrient waters with low turbidity. High nutrient levels reduce their competitive advantage over benthic algae and hence reduce coral reef integrity and diversity. In the Caribbean it has been shown that land use changes and subsequent increased sediment loadings, often exacerbated by seasonal storms, have resulted in the degradation of reef systems (for example, in St Lucia and Costa Rica: Cortes and Risk, 1985; Nowlis and others, 1997).

Given the complexity of related fringing mangrove, seagrass and reef systems in the BRMP, a meaningful water quality indicator was required that could be easily measured and projected across the scenarios. Nitrate concentration was adopted as an indicator of enhanced algal growth and nutrient loading. There is evidence in Buccoo Reef and elsewhere of a correlation between nitrate loading and other major pollutants. Kumarsingh and others (1998) examined phosphorus concentrations in sediments using coral coring methods and found that levels of phosphorus at BRMP were rising, although they were still lower than they had been in the early 1970s before the introduction of enhanced waste-water treatment facilities and the decline of the livestock sector. Levels of hydrocarbons, probably associated with fugitive emissions from recreational and commercial boats, were also high in the lagoon area of BRMP (Rajkumar and Persad, 1994). These high concentrations were observed despite this area being largely protected from other major sources of marine hydrocarbon contamination, such as the heavy oil tanker traffic to the east of Tobago.

The impact of the development scenarios on water quality, as reflected by nitrate concentrations, was estimated in two stages. First, the observed mean concentrations across marine-based observation points in Buccoo Reef were attributed to the terrestrial population contributing to this contamination. From this, per capita concentration factors were estimated for the total resident and tourist populations in the areas flowing into Buccoo Reef. Humans create the greatest proportion of nutrient loading in coastal seas. Howarth and others (1996) estimate that nitrate loadings from humans into the Atlantic and surrounding seas are of the order of 3.3–4.4kg per person per year. And the richer we are, the more we pollute. Concentration factors per capita were then multiplied by the extrapolated population projections to 2007 to arrive at the projected ambient concentrations in Table 5.5. 'Enhanced environmental management' (scenarios B and D) in this case refers to increased proportions of waste treated to tertiary level. As indicated in Table 5.1, the installation and adoption of tertiary-level treatment by the surrounding villages with a small per-household connection cost leads to projections of adoption of 50 and 70 per cent respectively for scenarios B and D.

Water quality is an important issue as it is also linked to the other ecological criteria, particularly seagrass productivity (measurable indicator 7) and coral reef quality (measurable indicator 8). Data on seagrass health and coral reef quality were collected as part of the research effort on Buccoo Reef, and analysis was undertaken building on existing data for Buccoo Reef (Woodley, 1997; Brown and others, 1999). The data on seagrasses show the expected correlation between nitrate levels and seagrass productivity, and extrapolation from these trends gives the estimates of seagrass productivity for 2007 in Table 5.5. For coral reef quality, the key question is that of water quality, particularly eutrophication processes with coral cover (see, for example, Pastorok and Bilyard, 1985; Tomascik and Sander, 1985). Projections of trends in nitrate loadings to 2007 are used to predict the coral reef quality indicator, with the results shown in Table 5.5. Mangrove area projections (measurable indicator 9) were estimated from aerial photographs and specific development plans under the scenarios of extensive or limited development.

Table 5.5 summarizes the values and scores for each of the nine measurable indicators across the four development scenarios. A substantial research effort by researchers from a range of disciplines was required to arrive at this point, despite the many previous research efforts in the area. This table does not, however, make decisions for us. It does not indicate which development scenario is preferred. The most preferred scenario is the one that achieves the highest score across the criteria. To enable the comparison of scenarios across

Table 5.5 *Estimated impacts of four development scenarios for Buccoo Reef Marine Park area on the economic, social and ecological criteria*

Criteria	Scenario			
	A	B	C	D
Economic				
(1) Economic revenues to Tobago (US$m)	9	11	17	19
(2) Visitor enjoyment of BRMP (US$m)	1.2	2.5	0.9	1.7
Social				
(3) Local employment (number of jobs)	2500	2600	6400	6500
(4) Informal sector benefits (score)	5	4	3	2
(5) Local access (score)	6	5	6	7
Ecological				
(6) Water quality (μg N/l)	1.5	1.4	2.2	1.9
(7) Seagrass health (g dry weight/m^2)	18	19	12	15
(8) Coral reef viability (% live stony coral)	19	20	17	18
(9) Mangrove health (ha)	65	73	41	65

Notes: scenarios are:
A: Limited tourism development without complementary environmental management
B: Limited tourism development with complementary environmental management
C: Expansive tourism development without complementary environmental management
D: Expansive tourism development with complementary environmental management

all criteria, the measurable indicator values are converted to scores and stakeholder weights are applied. This can be achieved through the process described in the following section as part of the trade-off analysis.

USING MCA TO PREFERENCE RANK SCENARIOS

To compare scenarios, the data within the effects table (Table 5.5) need to be standardized and converted into scores. The method of conversion for each measurable indicator depends on whether it constitutes an improvement to the situation (a benefit) or a loss (a cost). Whether a change is an improvement or a loss ultimately depends on the objectives of the decision-makers. To illustrate, for the fifth measurable indicator, local access to the coastal zone, if the MCA were being undertaken for a conservation agency, greater access by local people could be considered a loss as it could be damaging to the resource. Therefore local access would be a cost indicator, for which higher values reflect a deteriorating situation. If, on the other hand, ensuring local people have access to the coastal zone is an objective of the decision-maker, then it would be a benefit indicator for which higher values reflect an improvement.

Box 5.1 Scaling a benefit indicator: converting macroeconomic revenue values to scores

The macroeconomic benefits to Tobago were estimated by aggregating the potential net revenues that could accrue from visitor expenditure within Tobago over a ten-year period under the four alternative future scenarios described. The estimated benefits ranged from US$9 million to 19 million. This information is displayed in the effects table (Table 5.5).

To convert the four values (US$9 million, $11 million, $17 million and $19 million) into scores requires two steps. The first step assigns the score of 100 to the most preferred value – US$19 million is scored at 100. The next step scores the least preferred value at 0 – US$9 million is scored 0. The middle values (US$11 million and $17 million) are converted into scores using the formula:

$$X_s = \frac{x - x_{min}}{x_{max} - x_{min}} \times 100$$

where:

X_s = scored value
x = the value being transformed into a score
x_{max} = maximum value (= 19)
x_{min} = minimum value (= 9)

For the macroeconomic benefits indicator values (9, 11, 17 and 19) the final scores are therefore 0, 20, 80 and 100.

Once it is clear for each measurable indicator whether a higher or a lower value is preferred, each set of indicator values is scaled from 0 to 100. The least preferred outcome is assigned a value of 0, the most preferred outcome is assigned a value of 100. The values in between are ascribed scores relative to their distance from the upper limit of 100 and the lower limit of 0. Different methods are used to score the values depending on whether the most preferred outcome is the highest value (a benefit) or the lowest value (a cost). Both methods are described in Boxes 5.1 and 5.2.

In the case of a cost indicator, high values indicate less preferred outcomes. This is the case in the example below, where the indicator concerning nitrate levels in the coastal waters of the BRMP is converted into scores. Here the scores reflect that the most preferred outcome is the lowest value (see Box 5.2). Once the measurable indicator values have been converted into scores, the values can be replaced within the effects table by the scores. For each indicator the most preferred and least preferred outcomes can clearly be seen, the least preferred outcomes have a 0 value and the most preferred have a value of 100 (see Table 5.6).

If a decision were to be based solely on one measurable indicator, Table 5.6 shows which scenario would be preferred. For example, if the only important criterion were maximizing macroeconomic benefits, scenario D would be preferred. However, in terms of minimizing nitrates in coastal waters, scenario

---

BOX 5.2 SCALING A COST INDICATOR: CONVERTING WATER QUALITY VALUES TO SCORES

The water quality around the BRMP was estimated from samples taken from 20 marine and freshwater sites around the park. Using estimates of the possible level of water treated to tertiary level (described in the alternative future scenarios in Table 5.1), the likely changes in levels of nitrates in coastal waters under the alternative scenarios were estimated. The estimated range of values is: 1.4, 1.5, 1.9 and 2.2 μgl^{-1}. In this range, the highest level of nitrates was 2.2 μgl^{-1}. From the four values, the highest concentration is the least desirable level of water quality, and hence is assigned a score of 0. The lowest expected level of nitrates is 1.4 μgl^{-1}, indicating better water quality, thus scoring 100. The nitrate values in between, 1.5 and 1.9 μgl^{-1}, are converted into scores using the formula:

$$ x_s = \frac{x_{max} - x}{x_{max} - x_{min}} \times 100 $$

where:

x_s = scored value
x = the value being transformed into a score
x_{max} = maximum value (= 2.2)
x_{min} = minimum value (= 1.4)

For the water quality indicator values (1.4, 1.5, 1.9 and 2.2) the final scores using this method are therefore: 100, 88, 38 and 0, respectively. The conversion of water quality data from actual values to scores is shown thus:

	Score		Water quality data (μgl^{-1})
Most preferred	100	–	1.4
	88	–	1.5
	38	–	1.9
Least preferred	0	–	2.2

B would be preferred. To identify the future scenario that is most preferred, the impacts of all the criteria have to be taken into account. This is achieved by calculating mean scores for each criteria group and then taking an average of these scores (see Box 5.3). This process generates one final score for each scenario, which permits the ranking of the four scenarios. The scenario with the highest overall average score is considered the most preferred, and the scenario with the lowest score is the least preferred. The final preference rankings do not indicate by how much one scenario is preferred to another.

Table 5.6 *The scored effects of scenarios on economic, social and ecological criteria for Buccoo Reef*

| Criteria | Scenario | | | |
	A	B	C	D
Economic				
(1) Economic revenues to Tobago	0	20	80	100
(2) Visitor enjoyment of BRMP	19	100	0	50
Average score	*10*	*60*	*40*	*75*
Social				
(3) Local employment	0	3	98	100
(4) Informal sector benefits	100	67	33	0
(5) Local access	50	0	50	100
Average score	*50*	*23*	*60*	*67*
Ecological				
(6) Water quality	88	100	0	38
(7) Seagrass health	86	100	0	43
(8) Coral reef viability	67	100	0	33
(9) Mangrove health	75	100	0	76
Average score	*79*	*100*	*0*	*48*
Overall average score	**46**	**61**	**33**	**63**

DERIVING STAKEHOLDER WEIGHTS

The modelling part of the trade-off analysis described above is an entry point into stakeholder-led negotiations about priorities for management. The set of systematically ordered information for the MCA is used to engage stakeholder groups and explore their priorities. An iterative process began with each of the stakeholder groups meeting separately to discuss the management issues relating to Buccoo Reef. Finding common ground, even within groups identified as single stakeholders or entities, is often a resource-intensive activity in itself. In the case of Buccoo Reef it meant overcoming ongoing tensions within the organization of reef tour operators (Box 5.4) and recognizing the political realities of democratic structures, such as local councils.

The second stage involved each of the groups being presented over subsequent months with the outcome of their own deliberations and those of the other stakeholder groups, thereby challenging their preconceptions as to how others perceived the management issues. The final stage of this process involved the stakeholders coming together in a series of consensus-building workshops. Meetings with individual stakeholders built trust around the concepts and procedures of negotiation and validated local knowledge of the reef system and the ecological linkages in coastal areas. This trust in the process was vital in enabling the groups to come together.

The stakeholder groups included fishers, local communities, local businesses and entrepreneurs, reef tour and water-sports operators, recreational users and technical personnel from various departments of the Tobago House of

---

Box 5.3 IDENTIFYING THE SCENARIO THAT BEST MAXIMIZES
BENEFITS AND MINIMIZES COSTS

Having defined the impacts of each of the scenarios on the criteria in the effects table (see Table 5.5), and converted all the criteria values into scores (see Boxes 5.1 and 5.2), it is possible to identify the most desirable scenario. 'Most desirable' in this case means the scenario in which the benefits are maximized and the costs are minimized. Identifying that scenario involves estimating mean average scores for each of the scenarios. The mean scores of the evaluation criteria – economic, social and ecological – are calculated by averaging the scores of the measurable indicators within each group (see Table 5.6). For example, the mean value for the economic criteria:

under scenario A is: $(0 + 19) / 2 = 10$
under scenario B is: $(20 + 100) / 2 = 60$
under scenario C is: $(80 + 0) / 2 = 40$
under scenario D is: $(100 + 50) /2 = 75$

Repeating this exercise for the social and ecological criteria generates average scores for each criteria group under each scenario (see the 'average score' rows in Table 5.6).

Taking an average of the averages from the economic, social and ecological criteria produces an overall average score. This score will lie between 0 and 100 for each scenario. For example, the overall score for:

Scenario A is: $(10 + 50 + 79) /3 = 46$
Scenario B is: $(60 + 23 +100) /3 = 61$
Scenario C is: $(40 + 60 + 0) /3 = 33$
Scenario D is: $(75 + 67 + 47) /3 = 63$

The most preferred scenario can be identified from Table 5.6 as the column with the highest overall score in the bottom row. It can be seen that the overall average scores generate the following ranking of scenarios, from most to least preferred: D, B, A, C. The most desirable scenario is scenario D with an overall average score of 63. The close overall average scores for the top-ranking scenario D (score 63) and the second-ranking scenario B (score 61) needs some explanation. The method of averaging the scores generates an ordinal scale. This means that it cannot be inferred from the overall average scores by how much one scenario is better than another scenario. The only inference that can be made here is that scenario D is preferred to scenario B. It is not possible to say by how much.

Assembly (THA). As discussed in Chapter 4, stakeholder groups are not best represented in focus groups. The priorities of THA and park regulators were derived through a series of informant interviews and participatory exercises, including ranking exercises. The interests of the tourists and recreational users, an important stakeholder group affecting the financial sustainability of the island economy, could not be engaged easily in focus groups. A series of questions were added to the contingent valuation survey to reveal their priorities and preferences.

In the first and second stages of the process stakeholders were asked to give weighted priorities to various criteria for making decisions about future

Table 5.7 *Characteristics of nominal, ordinal, interval and ratio data*

Scale	Description	Examples
Nominal	Classifies data into mutually exclusive categories that can be used for identification purposes. It is a naming device only. The information generated cannot be manipulated statistically beyond computation of modal average.	Gender (male/female) Country of residence Occupation User/non-user Social security numbers
Ordinal	Ranks information into ordered groups, where higher group numbers indicate more of the group characteristic. This type of data is more easily manipulated than nominal data. Median and modal averages can be estimated although some statistics cannot be estimated.	Level of education Difficulty level of tests Consumer brand preference
Interval	Ranks information into ordered groups, with equal intervals between groups. There is no absolute zero point. Interval data is a more advanced level of measurement than ordinal data and can be added and subtracted.	Temperature scale
Ratio	This is the most advanced form of measurement, and is an interval scale with an absolute zero point. All arithmetic operations are possible and magnitudes can be compared.	Kilograms (mass) Currency Probability

development options. The weights were derived through focused and structured discussions about the implications of the scenarios and options for the management of Buccoo Reef and development in south-west Tobago. Stakeholders' preferences for different management priorities can be elicited in various ways. The method of eliciting information very often determines the format of the information. All information on preferences is either nominal, ordinal, interval or ratio data (see Table 5.7). The different types of information permit different levels and types of analysis.

Ideally, the most descriptive measurement should be used when estimating weights. The nominal scale is the least descriptive scale and the ratio scale is the most descriptive. More descriptive data permit more accurate comparisons and more detailed conclusions to be drawn. By way of illustration, the example in Box 5.3 used an ordinal scale of measurement and hence it was not possible to say by how much scenario D was preferred to scenario B. On the practical side, it is often the case that eliciting more descriptive data necessitates a more detailed and complex question for the respondent. Tables 5.8 to 5.11 provide examples of how to collect the four different types of data. Collecting nominal data is the easiest course for the respondents, as questions only require a 'yes' or 'no' response (see Table 5.8). For example, a respondent either considers a management option important or they do not. Ordinal data are recorded in the form of scales. The ordered preferences of respondents are measured in relation to a created scale. Table 5.9 shows that respondents can rank their

---

**BOX 5.4 GETTING THE BUCCOO REEF TOUR OPERATORS
TO ATTEND A MEETING**

The reef tour operators were unique among the interested economic stakeholders of Buccoo Reef in that they had an established forum for collective action: the Buccoo Reef Tour Operators' Cooperative. The purpose of the cooperative was to enable the reef tour operators to meet to discuss common issues. A dispute had previously developed between the members over where to base the central collection and drop-off point for the reef tour. Half the group departed from Buccoo village and half from Store Bay (see Figure 4.2 in Chapter 4). Each half aligned their preferences to the location that would maximize their own financial benefit. As a result of this rift the group rarely met, and when it did the dispute over the central collection point would dominate discussions.

After making initial contact with reef tour operators from Buccoo and Store Bay, further encounters were arranged to discuss the possible gains from their attendance and participation in a series of meetings about future options for Buccoo Reef. Each individual member of the reef tour operators was approached separately and invited to attend a meeting. After three or four visits to each reef tour operator and a reminder to each on the day of the first meeting, 15 operators attended the first stakeholder meeting. Even though this was a relatively large number for the focus groups (other stakeholder groups were restricted to eight to ten people) we did not turn anyone away.

---

preferences according to the scale given, where 1 indicates the highest preference.

Interval data also reflect ordered preferences in relation to a created scale. However, unlike ordinal scales, the interval scale has equal intervals between the groups. Table 5.10, which could be used to collect interval data, requires respondents to think more clearly about their relative preferences and requires them to indicate the relative size of their preferences. Ratio data, which reflect absolute values and hence can be used to reflect absolute differences between preferences, are collected using the most complicated form of question. To complete Table 5.11, the respondent must consider their absolute preferences for each of the management options. This is more difficult than merely stating that you prefer one option to another. Some respondents may find it difficult to place ratio values on their preferences because they are not familiar with thinking about their preferences in this way.

A fundamental problem in aggregating many people's preferences arises from the assumption that the preference units used (be they monetary values or votes) have the same real value for everyone. Even money has problems as a unit of measurement. By way of example, it is worth considering the value that a poor person places on US$100 relative to the value of US$100 to a rich person. This comparison is made clearer if you think of one person as a millionaire and the other as a pauper. In this case, the assumption of equal value does not hold (Goodwin and Wright, 1991).

If preferences are measured by votes instead of money or prices, there are still difficulties. If one respondent allocates 50 points to ecological criteria, 25 to economic criteria and 25 to social criteria we have to assume that this person

Table 5.8 *Example of a question to collect nominal data*

Question: Which of the following management options are important to you?
Tick (✔) all that apply.

Management options	Tick
Economic	
Social	✔
Ecological	✔

Table 5.9 *Example of a question to collect ordinal data*

Question: What priority do you think each of the following management options should be given by the government?
Assign the value '1' to the issues that should be tackled first, '2' to the issues that should be tackled second and '3' to the issues that should be tackled last.

Management options	Rank (1, 2 or 3)
Economic	2
Social	1
Ecological	1

Table 5.10 *Example of a question to collect interval data*

Question: How important are each of the following management options (economic, social, ecological) to you?
Indicate how important they are by ticking (✔) the appropriate box for each option.

Management options	Not at all important	Of small importance	Quite important	Very important
Economic		✔		
Social				✔
Ecological				✔

Table 5.11 *Example of a question to collect ratio data*

Question: How much priority do you think each of the management options should be given by the government?
Divide 100 points among the three options to show how much priority should be given to each issue (if you feel one should be given no priority, allocate no points to it).

Management options	Allocate all 100 points
Economic	20
Social	40
Ecological	40

values the environment twice as highly as either economic or social issues. If another person allocates 34 points to ecological, 33 to economic and 33 to social, they have the same preference order as the previous person, but their preferences for the environment are not as strong. Adding numerical values that people perceive differently (whichever unit is used) is a fundamental problem in aggregating preferences, and one that has not been satisfactorily resolved.

A variety of data were collected from the Buccoo Reef stakeholders to elicit their weights. In the first stakeholder meeting, the Buccoo Reef tour operators were asked to prioritize the main management issues for BRMP. Each stakeholder was given a voting form and was asked to vote in one of three ways. First, they were asked to indicate on their ballot which one of the three evaluation criteria (economic, social and ecological) they considered a priority for managers. This was undertaken to focus the minds of the group on the issues that they felt needed immediate action and it generated nominal data.

Participants were then asked to rank the three evaluation criteria. They were asked to place a '1' beside the criteria of most importance to them, a '2' next to the criteria of secondary importance and a '3' next to the criteria of tertiary importance. Stakeholders were asked, as far as possible, not to give two or three criteria the same rank. Finally, participants were asked to allocate ten votes to each of the specific measurable indicators. In this way the stakeholders were given a chance to allocate up to ten votes to as many measurable indicators they felt were important to them. The stakeholders were then asked if they wanted to change their initial ranking for the economic, social and ecological criteria.

The most important part of this process was the ranking of the three evaluation criteria. However, in allocating votes to specific measurable indicators the stakeholders were forced to think about relative priorities. The voting process revealed that each group of stakeholders prioritized ecosystem health, and that livelihoods and long-term economic prosperity depended on its maintenance. The discussions that occurred concurrently with the voting revealed considerable consensus as to the long-term priorities for managing BRMP. Table 5.12 shows the outcome of exercises undertaken in the six focus group consultations as well as scores revealed in the tourist survey. The figures are derived from the discussions and agreements between participants within each stakeholder group.

IDENTIFYING A WEIGHTED RANKING OF THE FUTURE SCENARIOS

Within MCA, there are two levels at which weights can be applied: the evaluation criteria level and the measurable indicators level. Applying weights to the evaluation criteria reveals the management priorities among these criteria. Applying weights to the measurable indicators can be undertaken to reflect their relative importance within the evaluation criteria groups. Weights are numbers that can be attached to items in order to represent their relative importance.

The Buccoo Reef example described here deals with the allocation of weights only at the criteria level. If weights are also applied at the measurable indicators level, the same principles (described below) apply. The actual application of weights to the MCA model is a straightforward process whereby the weights (in percentages) are multiplied by the scores.

Table 5.12 *Stakeholder weighting of priorities for management of Buccoo Reef Marine Park*

Priorities for manage- ment	Bon-Accord village council	Buccoo village council	Depts of the Tobago House of Assembly*	Fishers	Recreational users**	Reef tour operators	Watersports/ dive operators
Economic growth	22	25	19	18	9	27	23
Social issues	32	35	29	40	32	32	15
Ecosystem health	47	40	52	43	59	42	63

Notes: The figures in the table were derived by asking stakeholders to demonstrate preferences by allocating ten votes between three priorities for management (economic growth, social issues, ecosystem health). Weights were derived from focus group discussions and participatory allocation procedures except where stated.
* The THA was consulted through semi-structured interviews with individuals in different departments.
** Recreational users' preferences were derived from a sample survey of 1000 users of Buccoo Reef Marine Park in 1997.

To illustrate the impact of different stakeholders' management priorities on the ranked outcomes, a set of weights from a stakeholder with a strong preference for prioritizing social issues are multiplied by the scored values in Table 5.6, as shown in Table 5.13. The weights for a stakeholder who is interested in social improvement and ecosystem health but has less concern for direct economic issues might be as follows:

economic issues: 5 per cent
social issues: 55 per cent
ecological issues: 40 per cent
total: 100 per cent

Table 5.13 *Summary effects table showing weighted scores*

| Criteria | Scenarios | | | |
	A	B	C	D
Economic	1 (0.05 x 10)	3 (0.05 x 60)	2 (0.05 x 40)	4 (0.05 x 75)
Social	28 (0.55 x 50)	13 (0.55 x 23)	33 (0.55 x 60)	37 (0.55 x 67)
Ecological	32 (0.40 x 79)	40 (0.40 x 100)	0 (0.40 x 0)	19 (0.40 x 48)
Total	61	56	35	60

Note: weighted scores are in parentheses

To identify the preference ranking of the weighted future scenarios, the scores under each scenario are added together:

Scenario A: 1 + 28 + 32 = 61
Scenario B: 3 + 13 + 40 = 56
Scenario C: 2 + 33 + 0 = 35
Scenario D: 4 + 37 + 19 = 60

Using the sample set of weights, which gives high priority to the improved management of social issues and ecological interests but lower priority to economic issues, Scenario A (with the highest score) is the most preferred. It is important to note here the impact of including weights in the model, as it changes the most preferred outcome from Scenario D (see Table 5.6).

The stakeholder group meetings culminated in a workshop to bring different stakeholders together to resolve resource conflicts and build consensus on management strategies and development options for the management of the marine park. This was where the stakeholders could discuss the priorities for decision-making, see how they resulted in different impacts and development scenarios and then make consensus-based decisions about future action by trading-off the priorities for economic growth, social issues and ecosystem health. The outcome of these meetings was a set of firm proposals for action by individuals, the stakeholder groups and by the park regulators. The consensus-building processes are described in Chapter 6.

The evaluation of the scenarios through their impacts on the criteria, as shown in the effects table (Table 5.5), is the first step in the MCA and generates an ordered ranking of the development scenarios. The highest-scoring scenario can be considered the most desirable. Figure 5.2 shows the rank ordering of scenarios for a range of stakeholder preferences. These are compared to a base case of equal weighting of economic, social and ecological criteria. All the Buccoo Reef stakeholders in effect demonstrated concern for proactive management and limits on the development of south-west Tobago. Scenario B is ranked highest across the range of weightings (other than equal ranking).

There are differences, however, between the stakeholder weightings in the subsequent ordering of scenarios. For Buccoo Reef, more emphasis is placed by both the regulators and recreational users on ecosystem health than on economic criteria; this results in preferences for limitations to be placed on tourism development unilaterally (Scenario B is higher ranked than Scenario A in the regulators' and recreational users' rows in Figure 5.2). For local stakeholders, the implication of their prioritizing criteria is that they favour enhanced environmental management but prioritize harmonious economic and social development. This difference in priorities was substantiated by discussions in stakeholder meetings and at consensus-building workshops. Water quality in particular is directly linked to local stakeholders' perceptions of ecosystem integrity and quality of life.

Using the trade-off analysis approach means not only that stakeholders can be explicit about their priorities in decision-making, but that they can also see the potential outcomes and impacts in terms of the ranking of development scenarios, as portrayed in Figure 5.2, based on these priorities. In this way they can be informed about the trade-offs inherent in decisions about resource use and management.

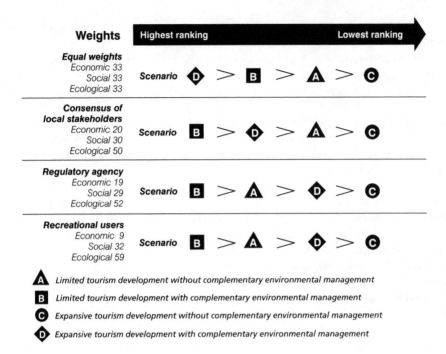

| Weights | Highest ranking | | | Lowest ranking |

Equal weights
Economic 33
Social 33
Ecological 33

Scenario D > B > A > C

Consensus of local stakeholders
Economic 20
Social 30
Ecological 50

Scenario B > D > A > C

Regulatory agency
Economic 19
Social 29
Ecological 52

Scenario B > A > D > C

Recreational users
Economic 9
Social 32
Ecological 59

Scenario B > A > D > C

A Limited tourism development without complementary environmental management

B Limited tourism development with complementary environmental management

C Expansive tourism development without complementary environmental management

D Expansive tourism development with complementary environmental management

Figure 5.2 *Rank ordering of development scenarios by Buccoo Reef stakeholders*

APPLYING TRADE-OFF ANALYSIS

This worked example of the MCA and stakeholder identification shows how trade-off analysis can be used to bring together diverse quantitative and qualitative information for decision-making to rank development scenarios on the basis of stakeholder values. The data for the case of BRMP show that there are trade-offs between expansive tourism development, which threatens the integrity of the coral reef through eutrophication, and more limited tourism development, which maintains fringing mangrove and seagrass areas. Engagement with stakeholder groups provides information on their explicit priorities and allows these groups to move beyond short-term conflicts over resource use. By informing all stakeholders about the implications of resource use and the acceptability of changing practices, directly resolving conflicts between users of the resource and building trust between the stakeholders, it was possible for the stakeholders themselves to have an input into the management of coastal and marine resources. Working closely with the regulatory agency and decision-makers within the responsible government agencies enables stakeholders to use their collective voice to urge action, and also demonstrates that regulators are engaged and willing to respond. This represents a departure from traditional top–down protected area management, but one which is necessary given the general failure of approaches to protect areas based on the exclusion of stakeholders.

Trade-off analysis represents the implementation of a constructive approach to decision-making, more widely applicable to MPAs, development planning and natural resource management. The inclusion of stakeholder views and values within a rigorous framework can, potentially, provide rich information for regulators seeking to manage marine park resources in partnership with other stakeholders. It provides, as suggested by Joubert and others (1997), a structure for public participation and the political accountability of such processes. We believe that participatory approaches are complementary to decision-support tools such as MCA, but are constrained by institutional circumstances. We take up this theme in the next chapter.

Trade-off analysis provides a framework that incorporates indicators of economic, social and ecological quality as well as stakeholder preferences. It is flexible enough to be modified as stakeholders' preferences develop and evolve, or as new scientific or social information becomes available. Its end use can only be determined by the users and participants in the process. Trade-off analysis produces a ranking of potential future scenarios by stakeholders, or their agreement to support certain management decisions. It can be reapplied iteratively over time and as information and preferences change, in order to keep the decision-makers informed about the impacts of management decisions and the level of stakeholder support. Alternatively, the tool could be used to support a move away from centralized decision-making towards collective action by local stakeholders or collaborative approaches, possibly in the form of co-management of the resource.

The application of trade-off analysis has identified a number of key lessons that indicate the central roles of knowledge and communication and the relationships between the resource managers and the stakeholders. Positivist scientific approaches that require the separation of the actors involved in research from the object under investigation are not possible when the researcher needs to build and maintain trusting relationships with the research participants at the same time. Hence, a constructive approach is needed to enable both researchers and participants to interact and engage in a dialogue, and to enable the research process to evolve as additional information is generated. The trade-off analysis process – through the interweaving of deliberative processes, impact assessment and consensus-building – creates an arena within which deliberation and analysis can coexist and contribute to management decision-making.

The evidence from the Buccoo Reef study indicates that participatory processes can be successful in developing supported environmental management strategies, although much emphasis is placed on the flexibility of the regulatory agency and its willingness to engage in and sustain the process. The level of government support could be a key factor in the success or failure of the approach. Chapter 6 discusses further procedural stages and institutional issues in trade-off analysis, showing how the techniques can be applied to build consensus and transform institutions for more integrated and inclusionary coastal management.

Chapter 6

Building Successful Institutions

Trade-off analysis provides a set of techniques and a framework to support inclusive and integrated coastal zone management. It explicitly includes a wide range of stakeholders and their diverse interests, views, knowledge and values in decision-making. It integrates a range of perspectives on coastal resources and evaluates the impacts of different courses of action on different aspects of the economy, ecosystems and society. Trade-off analysis is therefore both a constructive approach, and has the characteristics of a soft systems approach. It overcomes barriers to communication and encourages stakeholders to interact to support decisions as an integral part of coastal decision processes. Trade-off analysis also promotes social learning – how individuals learn to behave and use knowledge in social environments through interaction and deliberation. Building trust and openness, information-sharing and giving stakeholders positive reinforcing feedback are important elements in reducing communication barriers. But, in addition, empowerment can be promoted through opening channels of communication and validating lay input into the process. This chapter explores some of the contextual factors and prerequisites for empowerment and the implementation of a citizen-oriented science for the application of trade-off analysis. First we discuss using the techniques of trade-off analysis as part of conflict-resolution and consensus-building processes. We then discuss the broader institutional factors that support or constrain the application of trade-off analysis and the development of more inclusionary and integrated approaches to natural resource and environmental management. Much of this institutional analysis is illustrated, once more, with respect to Trinidad and Tobago.

MANAGING CONFLICT, BUILDING CONSENSUS

What is conflict?

Conflict exists in our everyday lives. It arises wherever there are competing objectives for the same good, service or outcome. Thus most economic activities, formal party politics and the politics of the everyday generate conflict. On the one hand, the process of conflict can lead to rivalry, quarrels and mistrust that can jeopardize development opportunities and potential. On the other hand, conflict can, in non-violent settings, act as the catalyst for positive social change (Warner, 2000). There are, of course, diverse theoretical perspectives (from Marx to Freud) on the role of conflict and violent conflict in shaping cultures, histories and societies. But at its simplest, from the perspective of the behavioural sciences, Moore (1986) captures the essence of conflict thus:

> *All societies, communities, organizations and interpersonal relationships experience conflict at one time or another in the process of day-to-day interaction. Conflict is not necessarily bad, abnormal or dysfunctional, it is a fact of life* (Moore, 1986, cited in Rijsbersman, 1999, p10).

In sociology, psychology and the behavioural sciences, much effort has been put into conflict management. Conflict is often described as a process that occurs in several stages. Conflict can be latent and occurs where there are, for example, scarce resources with competing interests. Second, perceived conflict leads to stress, tension and hostility. Recognizing the existence of conflict can lead to actual behavioural changes ranging from passive resistance to overt aggression. This behavioural change often leads to some kind of conflict aftermath (Pondy, 1967; Minnery, 1985). Encompassing all these facets of conflict, Powelson (1972) suggests that conflicts are merely 'the joint action of two or more parties seeking inconsistent goals'.

To better understand the nature of the conflict, conflicts can be classified into four distinct types:

1   *Conflicts over information or facts.* These types of conflict can often be dealt with by collecting additional information.
2   *Conflicts over values or beliefs,* such as religious beliefs or cultural values. Where values or beliefs are firmly rooted there is often no possibility of conflict management and the only option is to agree to disagree.
3   *Conflicts about interpersonal relationships.* Relationship conflicts tend to develop when people compete for position and engage in posturing, whereby they stake personal reputations or pride on certain outcomes. Personality clashes between and within stakeholder groups can most often be resolved by neutral third party intervention.
4   *Conflicts over interests and needs.* This is the area where conflict management can play the most useful role.

There are many possible reactions to conflict. The conflict can be ignored or avoided by one or more party withdrawing from the conflict. Alternatively, the conflict can be managed, in which case it can either be suppressed or regulated (Dorow, 1981). Conflict management is a catch-all term that refers to all methods of handling conflict and resolving conflict situations. It is the application of mechanisms or procedures to a perceived conflict situation so as to achieve a desired end result (Minnery, 1985).

Understanding conflicts in the coastal zone

As we have seen already, coastal zone management can be hindered by a range of conflicts at many scales. At one level, for example, there is international disagreement over the responsibility of individual nations for human-induced climate change and for taking action to curb greenhouse gas emissions. This conflict impacts on coastal zones in a variety of ways, as outlined in Chapter 1, including raised probabilities of coral bleaching and the impacts of accelerated sea level rise. Local conflicts can occur on-site among users of coastal resources, such as tourists and fishers. Conflicts among national or international agents at the macro scale can be shown to stem from the geopolitics of the nation state. Equally, the conflicts can arise from a lack of clarity in management responsibility due to poorly structured institutional arrangements for management. This can contribute to limited or inadequate implementation of regulations. Micro-scale conflicts often arise as a result of inadequate information or conflicting facts over specific stakeholder interests or needs, as well as from the everyday politics of resource allocation. Institutional structures designed to exclude rather than include stakeholders, to withhold information and avoid communication within institutions and with other agents, exacerbate these problems.

Recognizing the type of problems that underlie conflicts at different scales is an important step towards resolving the conflicts. In terms of managing conflicts, approaches that facilitate the resolution of conflict by the stakeholders themselves, with as little external involvement as possible, tend to create the most enduring solutions but can be just as resource-intensive to facilitate (Rijsberman, 1999; Singleton, 2000). A central element in managing conflict at all scales involves removing the personal element from the conflict and looking at the needs and interests of all the groups engaged in the conflict (Fisher and Ury, 1982).

Conflicts of interest among agents who manage coastal resources commonly arise because of poorly defined management rights and responsibilities (Gezon, 1997). Inter-institutional conflict can be better understood through a stakeholder analysis of all the agents involved and their interests. Greater horizontal integration among policy-makers in the various departments involved in managing coastal resources may reduce the problems of inter-institutional conflict (Cicin-Sain, 1993). If each agency is clear about its role and its responsibilities in managing the coastal zone, and can communicate its interest to the other management agents, there may at least be a better understanding of the problems (Imperial, 1999).

The conflicts arising from inadequate information, both at the local level and between management agencies, may be resolved by compiling information and disseminating it to stakeholders. But before this can happen, and as we discussed in Chapter 4, there has to be an exploration of the interests and needs of the different stakeholders to determine who they are and their informational needs. Providing information alone may remove one element from the conflict, such as misunderstanding the impacts of decisions, although it may highlight another area, such as the distribution of costs of a decision.

As we have shown in the trade-off analysis approach, the provision of information to stakeholders should be tied to a programme of inclusion in decision-making and deliberation. Such a programme should provide the primary and secondary stakeholders with a forum in which to deliberate on both scientific information and other stakeholders' interests. This forum should offer stakeholders the opportunity to discuss priorities for management, ensure that they can receive feedback on their input, and enable them to become more involved in further information collection or resource management deliberation. Ultimately, this forum may evolve into a forum to discuss or promote community engagement in coastal zone management, or it may choose to disband. But as we have seen, the initial merit of a deliberative forum is that it opens a channel of communication between the stakeholders and the decision-makers (Steins and Edwards, 1999).

Managing conflict

Conflict management has to take into account the emotional states of those in the participatory process, specifically their levels of trust in and suspicion of both the process and other participants. The conflict management mountain in Figure 6.1 and described in Brown and others (1995) shows how cooperation can be built, but it is a long and often tortuous climb: no walking holiday. Ascending the mountain from base camp, conflict management processes move those in conflict from isolation or confrontation to cooperation. From a starting point of isolated stakeholders, where there is apathy and no stakeholder involvement, at the base of the left face of the mountain, the first consideration is how to bring stakeholders into the conflict management process. The first step is information sharing, which can improve communication and encourage collaboration. And so, the progress up the mountain continues towards cooperation.

Alternatively, from the starting point of confrontation, the first step could be to legislate to avoid civil disobedience and promote harmony. However, it should be noted that proceeding up this mountain from the left side or the right side does not necessarily involve taking all the steps that are relevant to the situation described by Brown and others (1995). The mountain is useful because it describes a wide range of steps that may be applied individually or together in conflict management. The framework also highlights that conflict management requires both faces of the mountain in Figure 6.1 to be addressed. The left face of the mountain is about building trust, empowering the participants and bringing the participants or stakeholders into the process. The right face is about negotiating and bargaining, and ensuring the participants remain engaged in the process. In any attempt at conflict management, both aspects may need to be implemented as different stakeholder groups or participants may feel that they are being confronted, are ready to confront an issue, or that they are isolated and excluded.

Conflict leads to isolation, apathy or even violent confrontation, a breakdown in communication between stakeholders, a loss of trust and a feeling of powerlessness, particularly for those isolated as a result of the conflict. Any

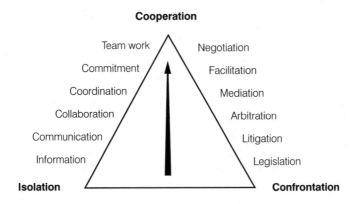

Figure 6.1 *The conflict management mountain*

conflict management process has therefore to address the issues of trust and power relationships. Simply defined, trust is a reliance on and confidence in the truth, worth and reliability of another with the goal or expectation that the parties in conflict will cooperate in the future (Pruitt and Carnevale, 1993).

Environmental planning and management conflicts are also exacerbated by stakeholders' divergent beliefs about the extent of the environment problem and the role of the management institutions (Lubell, 2000). This cognitive conflict is often based on a lack of knowledge and communication among stakeholders and institutions. Gregory and Keeney (1994) cite several examples of cases where a lack of shared understanding of the decision problem and of the impacts of the different management strategies exacerbated conflict among stakeholders, and created a loss of trust in the management agencies. Thus, loss of trust in the environmental management agency reduces the ability of any agency to manage (Beierle and Konisky, 2000).

But trust is fragile (Slovic, 2000, p503). It is difficult to develop and easy to destroy. This asymmetric shape of trust has long been recognized by psychologists but it appears to be intransigent. There is no fast way to rebuild trust in decision-making processes. One principle for rebuilding trust is, again, greater transparency through public input into decision-making, which can be achieved through various forms of participation and deliberation (Schneider and others, 1997). Raising awareness about existing levels of cooperation, and other stakeholders' willingness to participate, may help to reduce mistrust by building optimism about the process and generating greater levels of participation. Wider dissemination of information about the nature of the problem may also increase group cohesion as a necessary step towards trust. Thus, deliberative processes can form the foundations for cooperative rather than confrontational decision-making by enabling each stakeholder groups to understand the aims and perspectives of other groups and by enabling communication and the establishment of trusting relationships (Dryzek, 1997). Support for participatory processes at the political level and by other local organizations also play an important role in generating trust in decisions and management. This holds true in general and certainly for coastal management situations (Geoghegan and others, 1999).

The importance of trust-building and sharing knowledge of other groups' perceptions and needs among the stakeholder groups cannot, therefore, be underestimated (see also Liebman, 2000). Preferences evolve as new information feeds into the decision-making process. As stakeholders receive or acquire more information, once they assimilate it, their views and preferences may change (Crance and Draper, 1996). Without access to all available information stakeholders cannot make fully informed decisions. However, information has to be made available in ways that can be understood by all stakeholders.

The mere act of disseminating information about environmental change (as discussed by Liebman, 2000) may lead to some stakeholders developing or changing their views. If the dissemination is not followed up by discussion, however, the new information may be forgotten and discarded. Deliberation is, in essence, the act of carefully thinking something out in advance. Deliberation gives stakeholders the opportunity to develop their ideas through discussion and debate. A nurturing environment for deliberation also enables stakeholders to listen to and question other stakeholders' preferences and views.

A major benefit of deliberation is that it offers stakeholders the opportunity to validate their own knowledge, which, again, builds confidence and trust (O'Hara, 1996). In addition, by repeatedly articulating their preferences and discussing them openly, deliberation offers stakeholders the space to rehearse their ideas and find support for their perspectives. Having the chance to rehearse talking about issues in a supportive environment also gives less confident participants the opportunity to articulate their views in a coherent manner without being aggressive or emotional, and this enhances the credibility of what is said.

Conflict resolution and building consensus

Some conflicts resolve themselves, some come to a stalemate and some require arbitration. The necessary amount of external intervention is not given for any conflict and can range from a light touch to full-scale arbitration. At one end of the scale there is consensus-building involving minimum intervention from outside parties or stakeholders simply finding solutions among themselves. At the other end of the continuum represented in Figure 6.2, there is enforced arbitration, either through private arbitrators or the judicial system. The minimum intervention techniques are the least costly means of resolving conflict. As soon as outside arbitrators are involved, resource inputs increase substantially. The minimum intervention options are also the most manageable by coastal zone managers, who may not have a background in conflict management.

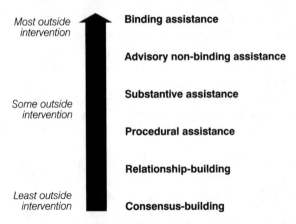

Most outside
intervention

Some outside
intervention

Least outside
intervention

Binding assistance

Advisory non-binding assistance

Substantive assistance

Procedural assistance

Relationship-building

Consensus-building

Figure 6.2 *Continuum of levels of intervention by a third party in conflict resolution activities*

It may not always be possible to minimize external intervention in conflict management. For example, fisheries disputes over territorial waters may need international arbitration. Trinidad and Barbados and a number of Caribbean islands have been in dispute over rights in the shared flying-fish fishery. In this case, international arbitration is a necessity. In the Buccoo Reef case, consensus-building techniques were most appropriate. It was possible to use these methods as the number of stakeholders involved in the Buccoo Reef study was relatively small. In addition, the groups were located within a few kilometres of each other and, most importantly, there were very clearly areas of agreement among stakeholders.

Empowering stakeholders to voice their views and building trust in the decision-making process can, however, take the process only to the point at which each stakeholder group recognizes the validity of their own and others' preferences and values. Disagreements may still exist among all the stakeholder groups about other management issues. Disagreements and dissent within society, it has been suggested, are addressed through three authorities: science, tradition and consensus (Moscovici and Doise, 1994). Where science cannot provide answers, and where traditions have broken down, it may be that only consensus-building remains to bring solutions and resolve disagreements.

How do we find consensus where there is none? One alternative is to propose a compromise through bargaining that is a move away from all the stakeholders' original positions. Another alternative is to exploit differences in stakeholders' perceptions of the likelihood of future scenarios occurring to develop contingency plans (Maguire and Boiney, 1994). Fisher and Ury (1982) suggest that there are four central principles in negotiations and finding consensus. First, separate the people from the problem. Second, focus on interests, not positions. Third, generate a variety of possibilities before deciding what to do. And fourth, insist that the result is based upon an agreed objective standard. These principles, rather than a blueprint, appear to be highly appropriate for conflict management in the coastal zone. They permit the consensus-building to evolve as necessary as stakeholders move towards more participatory approaches to conservation and development in the coastal zone.

The first stage, therefore, in separating the people from the problem is to assess the issues that are involved, the sources of the conflict, the people involved in the dispute, the nature of each group or individual's interests or concerns, the legal and institutional context and the stage of the conflict. The willingness of stakeholders to participate in a conflict management process must also be gauged. The central steps in assessing conflict are:

- notify individuals and stakeholder groups about what is planned, and the purpose of the exercise;
- arrange and manage stakeholder or group interviews; and
- ensure that the information collected in each stakeholder meeting is accurate and reflects stakeholders' views.

Working with focus groups, small groups and individual stakeholders opens channels of communication between stakeholder groups, and enables a sharing of knowledge between the groups about their needs, fears and values. Group work is useful to build trust and empower individuals and groups to become more active in decision-making. From the initial meetings with the stakeholder groups, the focus must be on drawing out the issues for resolution, namely, the conflicting interests among the different users of the resource. Steps should be taken to prevent discussions from descending into personal disputes or bargaining over individual positions.

There are typically strict hierarchies within stakeholder groups. These often prevent certain individuals from speaking openly. There may be effective taboos about certain subjects and there may be personality clashes. When discussions become heated and individuals start to stake their position, a neutral moderator is an effective means to move the issue back to the interests and needs of the stakeholders. By doing this repeatedly, the message is given that the object of consensus-building is resolving the problem, which is essentially what the stakeholders also want, not in airing personal feuds.

Most conflict management and consensus-building processes begin with sharing information and clarifying the aims and objectives of the process. Hence, the first aim of integrating conservation and development involves informing the coastal zone stakeholders of their shared needs for balancing the risks and benefits associated with both strategies. Public meetings ensure that awareness is raised about the planned process, that there is official support from the management agency and the decision-makers, that differing public and private perceptions of resource management issues are valid; and that issues of importance to the participants are clarified.

Once a series of smaller meetings have been held with individual stakeholder groups to work through the issues of concern, a consensus-building meeting can be held where the groups are brought together. This can be the culmination of this trust-building effort. Careful preparation before any consensus-building meeting can facilitate progress. In the case of Buccoo Reef, we facilitated a consensus-building workshop in 1999. The objectives and

Box 6.1 The consensus-building stakeholder meeting for Buccoo Reef

The objective of the meeting in March 1999 was to bring together primary stakeholders and to build consensus on management issues that had emerged from a year of ongoing debate and engagement. The workshop sought specifically to *identify three areas of consensus* between stakeholders as the starting points for setting management priorities for the resources associated with Buccoo Reef, and *identify three practical means of working towards achieving and implementing* decisions based on areas of consensus.

At the workshop, the stakeholders were asked to vote to identify their main areas of concern for the future of Buccoo Reef in terms of long-term challenges, medium-term planning issues and immediate problems. In each of these timeframes the stakeholders first of all identified and subsequently prioritized the challenges, issues and problems. The photograph shows the allocation of priorities by stakeholder representatives to alternative medium-term planning issues at the meeting. The vast majority of the stakeholder groups demanded immediate action on wastewater treatment for south-west Tobago. Wastewater was deemed to be a priority over regulations on land clearance or destruction of mangroves.

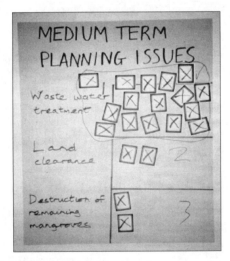

The stakeholders agreed that their priorities involved:

- dealing with the issues of limited awareness and knowledge of the environment of Tobago (the long-term challenge);
- the level of wastewater treatment (a medium-term planning issue);
- direct physical damage to the reef, ie reef-walking and anchoring (an immediate problem); and
- oil and gas pollution in the lagoon (an immediate problem).

The stakeholders also identified a number of actions that could be implemented by themselves, by their stakeholder group, by their community group or by the local government immediately, in the medium term and also in the longer term, to bring about change.

The consensus building process highlighted several important lessons for resource management.

- Sustainable management strategies involve building on the resources that people already have – local knowledge, experience and ideas. Concentrating on solutions that require financial or other resources that are in short supply will not bring about change. There are almost invariably opportunities to develop partnerships between local communities, stakeholder groups, government agencies and NGOs.
- Concentrate on what is achievable. Considering unrealistic solutions is a waste of limited resources when stakeholders are working together.
- Focus on the areas that have broad support. The consensus-building workshop proved that there are areas of agreement among the stakeholders. Taking action on those areas of agreement can lead to increased cooperation among the groups, and should motivate the groups to reach further agreement.

content of this workshop are summarized in Box 6.1. The preparation for such events involves showing the stakeholders courtesy and respect, and treating each of them as equals. To keep the balance there should be a similar number of participants invited from each stakeholder group, so that the members of one group do not outnumber any others. The participants should be informed about which other groups will be attending the meeting so that they are also prepared. The participants should also know in advance the purpose and objectives of the consensus-building meeting, so it is essential to distribute in advance a comprehensive agenda with clear time-guides for the meeting. In addition, it is useful to use an external facilitator, ideally someone who is respected and known locally to be unpartisan. All of these considerations, coupled with participatory techniques at the consensus-building meeting, should enable the stakeholders to find common ground and areas of agreement.

Role of trade-off analysis in conflict management

The application of trade-off analysis concurrently with conflict resolution and consensus-building approaches indicates some critical directions for integrated and inclusive coastal management. First, stakeholder analysis facilitates the understanding and analysis of the use and user conflicts that exist within the coastal zone. Second, we find that the perceived and actual coastal zone use conflicts can be recast conceptually in terms of 'important issues for management', as identified by each of the stakeholder groups. Working closely with the stakeholder groups over a period of time, using consensus-building and conflict management techniques, provides stakeholders with the opportunity to become engaged in the decision-making process. Using stakeholder-identified 'issues for management' to categorize use conflicts, stakeholder groups can be encouraged to deliberate on the importance of other stakeholders' needs and hence search for management options or approaches that might take into account most stakeholders' needs. Third, multi-attribute and multi-criteria analyses present clearly both scientific and value or qualitative information, thereby giving stakeholders a clear picture of the range of impacts of different management actions. Multi-criteria analysis (MCA) can reveal the nature of the trade-offs that generally exist between conservation and development, as well as more specifically the trade-offs between economic growth, social well-being and environmental health. The weighted ranked outcomes of an MCA can usefully be presented in open spaces such that stakeholders can reconsider the impacts of the decisions that they may prefer. Presenting the stakeholders with this information is important in gaining the stakeholders' trust, building their commitment to work with other stakeholders and engaging them in the decision-making process. Providing the space, both political and physical, for discussion and assimilation and to question both scientific and anecdotal information contributes to the development and articulation of stakeholder views. A clear articulation of group preferences can offer support to coastal zone management decision-making.

Inclusive, learning-based processes, which facilitate deliberation and participation, cannot, however, guarantee transparent, effective and supported decision-making. Environmental decision-making is often messy and contingent upon the intermingling of power, interests and chance (Parson and Clark, 1995). Nevertheless, the provision of an opportunity for social learning gives stakeholders the time and space they may need to consider methods for management and their own understanding of the opportunities that exist for alternative approaches. To develop the opportunities for resource management networks to form, spaces have to be identified and created in which the stakeholders can discuss and deliberate their issues of concern (Forester, 1999). Such deliberative spaces are most effective when they are fully backed by the decision-makers and local resource managers. Support in this context is manifested through to a willingness to use the deliberative spaces to learn about the various stakeholders' multiple and often conflicting views, share information and engage in an inclusive dialogue. Communication of information, interests and needs plays a central role in establishing such spaces. The institutional setting of deliberative processes is therefore of paramount importance for success in terms of process and outcomes.

BUILDING INSTITUTIONS FOR INCLUSIVE AND INTEGRATED MANAGEMENT

Collaboration and co-management

We have outlined some principles and contexts for managing conflicts between the goals of conservation and development. At the same time, the political and institutional context determines their ultimate success. The greater the depths of social networks, the greater the opportunities for social learning and hence the potential for the adoption of new institutional arrangements to promote and allow lasting impacts of consensus (Cox, 1998). When individuals spend time together to forge networks and open channels of communication, the relationships that are built can form the basis for the collective action highlighted in Chapter 2 as the central characteristic of coastal zone management. Collective action may then bring about changes that may not have arisen if any one individual had attempted the same action single-handedly (Ravnborg and Guerrero, 1999).

For coasts we should often be aiming for co-management. Co-management is a formal management system that falls between state management and community management. It involves active participation by the local community as well as intervention by the government, and devolution of power from the government to the local level (Lim and others, 1995). Characteristically, co-management approaches are initiatives that have formal organizational structures, but membership and leadership are participatory and control over decision-making can be either decentralized or central (Jentoft, 1989). One current focus of co-management is on identifying characteristics of regimes that ensure successful collaborative management (see, for example, Blumenthal and Jannick, 2000; Venter and Breen, 1998).

One of the central findings of research in this area is that co-management arrangements are most likely to evolve where there has been effective participation in decision-making. This completes the cycle we have described in this book from collective action to guided decision-making to co-management arrangements. Co-management requires the early involvement of stakeholders in decision-making, representative participants and an independent and unbiased process of participation. In addition, effective participation is reinforced if the outcomes of the participation have a perceptible and positive impact on the resources themselves (Rowe and Frewer, 2000). These conditions, coupled with the importance of open channels of communication and spaces for deliberation, suggest the need for platforms where complex natural resource management issues, such as coastal zone management, can be negotiated. Röling (1994) suggests that platforms for collective action are created when multiple stakeholders realize that they have the same resource management interests, that they have the influence to change one or more parts of the problem, and that they are willing to work together to solve the problem.

We have argued that the concept of integrated coastal zone management should be expanded to be more inclusive and to encompass deliberative processes. These processes should contribute to the development of four important aspects of coastal management. First, inclusion and deliberation should facilitate stakeholder understanding of the conflicts that exist, whether they are conflicts of interest, conflicts related to a lack of information, or conflicts related to a lack of understanding of the information. Second, deliberative and inclusionary processes can potentially provide the time and space for stakeholder learning and participation in decision-making. Third, such processes facilitate communication that can build trust and harmonize stakeholder knowledge about resource management. Fourth, inclusion and deliberation can lead to the evolution of a platform for collective action that offers the possibility for alternative institutions for coastal zone management, such as co-management arrangements.

Integration

Much of the research and emerging practice on coastal zone management nods in the direction of integrated or holistic approaches. The concept and meaning of integration has been widely debated (see, for example, Kenchington and Crawford, 1993). There is a growing understanding that integration refers to both horizontal integration across sectors and vertical integration across different scales (see Cicin-Sain, 1993; Clark, 1996). There is also support for the notion that integrated approaches should also be interdisciplinary (Turner, 2000) and combine understanding of land and marine use processes (Sorensen, 1997). By contrast, there has been little attention directed towards what we have emphasized in this chapter, namely the need for an inclusive approach that engages all levels of stakeholders and incorporates social and ecological resilience. The awareness of the need for inclusionary processes in resource management comes from experience elsewhere in integrating conservation and development in the context of land-based resources, protected areas and, to an extent, managing smaller coastal areas and marine parks (Agrawal and Gibson, 1999; Ticco, 1995; Alder, 1996).

The challenge for integrated coastal zone management therefore lies in developing an approach that is methodologically robust, transparent and understood by all stakeholders, that can build bridges between stakeholders, and that overcomes the sometimes severe barriers to collaborative management. Interdisciplinary approaches offer the greatest scope for advancement by drawing on a wide range of techniques to manage the conflicts and the diversity of uses of the coastal zone. The interaction between the elements within trade-off analysis ensures that it provides a horizontally integrated approach. Horizontal integration in this context refers to the inclusion of the multiple sectors involved in coastal zone management in the decision-making process. Clearly, stakeholder analysis is an important element in developing a horizontally integrated approach. Not only does it identify the powerful, influential and important multiple stakeholders, it also highlights the cross-sectoral range of stakeholder interests and, later, the stakeholders' collective values, as part of the conflict management process.

Vertical integration can be enhanced through the interaction of the stakeholder analysis and the technical decision-making process. The elicitation of stakeholders' preferences and values through deliberation and discussion ensures that the preferences of stakeholders at all scales, from the highest-level decision-makers to the on-site users, are incorporated. The elicited values, which are important in developing management priorities, contribute to the evolution of stakeholder knowledge and reinforce social learning in the stakeholder groups concerning other groups' views and the importance of local knowledge.

Using quantitative modelling techniques to complement the stakeholder analysis and consensus-building, scientific information can be channelled from specialists to local stakeholders and local knowledge can be channelled back into the decision-making process. Quantitative modelling also ensures that those stakeholders who place more value on scientific information than on local knowledge or deliberation and participation can be brought into the process.

Building relationships within the management institutions through consensus-building techniques with actors in economic planning, social services and marine resource management, increases the level of integration and inclusion. An important component of this consensus-building is the level of political will and support that is given to the process. The support of the decision-makers or policy-makers in one sense reveals their trust in the process. Without a completely inclusive process in which important stakeholders appear interested, the decision-makers may not be willing to support the process (Davos, 1998). Building trusting relationships with all stakeholders through maintaining an open dialogue, disseminating information and listening to their concerns has been shown to overcome this circular dilemma and to generate supported decisions. Thus, we would argue that including diverse values from the various stakeholder groups in the decision-making process is a prerequisite for integrated and inclusive coastal zone management. Indeed, to ensure that there is integrated conservation and development in the coastal zone a transparent framework in which to manage stakeholder conflicts is needed, where time and space are made for effective inclusion, deliberation and participation in the decision-making process.

CONSTRAINTS AND CHALLENGES TO INCLUSION AND INTEGRATION

Even with the most carefully designed and facilitated participatory process and the most sensitive conflict resolution, integration and inclusion are elusive. The mixed results from two decades of community participation in resource management suggest in general that it is ultimately constrained by the institutional arrangements, the legislative framework and the organizational skills of stakeholder communities. Social or cultural factors such as social class structures also play a central role in determining the scope of participatory or community-based coastal zone management. And, as we have pointed out earlier, community participation in coastal zone management may not by itself generate sustainable management. It is, of course, worth persisting. Community participation in decision-making appears to highlight local understanding of the resource use issues, empowers local groups, lessens conflicts and potentially musters support for various management alternatives that certainly are components of sustainability.

This section outlines some key thinking on the institutional components of the whole coastal management dilemma. We focus on the three levels of legal frameworks, organizations and power relations that pervade the institutional framework. We illustrate this once again with reference to Buccoo Reef in its wider context as a protected area within Trinidad and Tobago.

Barriers and bridges at Buccoo Reef

During 1999 and 2000, activities at Buccoo Reef of stakeholder involvement, public meetings and debate became widely reported in Trinidad and Tobago.

Was this a sign of something new in the ways things were done and in the relation between government and communities? Tobago continued to assert elements of autonomy in governance and planning, setting itself as distinct from national government in Port of Spain. The whole country considered further expansion of its network of terrestrial and marine protected areas to safeguard these unique resources for the future. Within this mêlée, typical of demands and trends in many countries, we began to research the question of why inclusive management was not being implemented for existing and proposed management conflicts. This was all the more dispiriting when it appeared to offer much promise.

To understand the structure and behaviour of coastal zone management institutions in Trinidad and Tobago we came to realize that we need to understand three scales: constitutional elements, including external factors, the policy, legal and regulatory setting; institutional and structural factors; and the operational arrangements and power relations. Within each of the three scales we consider in this section the type and strength of networks of dependence and exchange, and their roles in facilitating integrated and inclusive approaches to natural resource management. This framework enables us to assess the opportunities and constraints to public resource management within relevant institutions. We uncovered the relationships between these elements and began to understand the barriers and bridges (as Lance Gunderson and colleagues (1995) describe them) to inclusive management. We came to these relationships through systematic institutional research in 1999 and 2000. This involved talking to many individuals and to representatives of organizations throughout Trinidad and Tobago. It also involved talking to individuals in the region because some of the networks and institutional links stretched well beyond the shores of Trinidad and Tobago. The details of the research process and the in-depth review of institutional architecture can be found in Brown and others (2001) and in Tompkins and others (2002). This section concentrates on giving a flavour of what these institutional barriers and bridges are, and the lessons for wider inclusive coastal management, and the reconciliation of conservation and development. Table 6.1 shows the main issues identified by participants and respondents as affecting the development of an integrated and inclusive approach to natural resource management in Trinidad and Tobago.

External factors, national legislation and local legislation determine the constitutional elements of the institutional architecture of resource management in Trinidad and Tobago. External factors are those influences originating from outside Trinidad and Tobago, such as treaties that the government of Trinidad and Tobago has signed or conditions attached to loan agreements from external sources. Increasingly, external lending agencies are applying conditionality to both loans and grants, requiring host countries to pass certain legislation prior to drawing down loan funds.

Many of the laws currently in place in Trinidad and Tobago have not been updated since their creation under the British colonial system. Most of these old laws do not require public participation in decision-making for resource use or management, although there are a few exceptions. Despite some revisions to

Table 6.1 *Stakeholder perceptions of constraints to the development of integrated and inclusive coastal zone management in Trinidad and Tobago*

Institutional scale	Perceptions of constraints to development of an integrated and inclusive approach
Constitutional order	Existing legislation. External policy influences. Unclear roles of government departments and ministries. Legal liability of resource managers. Legal support for managers. Lack of co-management legislation. Unclear property rights. Legal protection for volunteers.
Organizational structure	Level of staff skill. Number of trained staff. Lack of previous successful examples. Credibility of the implementing agency. Hidden political agendas. Possible power loss by government agencies. Empowered staff. Local versus central government. Information hoarding. Project timetabling. Project cycle.
Operational arrangements	Representativeness. Level of communication. Level of law enforcement. Potential downsides to participation. Resource-intensive process. Stakeholder engagement guidelines. Intra-community relations.

Source: Tompkins and others (2002). Data derived from interviews with government, non-government and other stakeholders, Trinidad and Tobago, October–November 1999

some standard practices, there is still no explicit legislation that mandates stakeholder participation in decision-making about the environment or in developing new laws for the environment. There are several important gaps in the areas being tackled by new legislation (see Table 6.2), including clarification of rights of ownership of intertidal and other areas, and the definition of roles of voluntary wardens, for example.

Existing legislation in Trinidad and Tobago constrains the development of deliberative processes, or spaces of engagement as we have termed them in Chapter 2, in several ways. First, the legislation poorly defines the roles and responsibilities for managers of natural resources. In many cases different ministries have responsibility for the same resource. Three formal government agencies are currently responsible for the coastal resources in Tobago:

1   The Department of Fisheries and Marine Resources, Tobago House of Assembly, empowered by the minister responsible for Tobago's affairs.
2   The Department of Fisheries, in the Ministry of Agriculture, Lands and Marine Resources.
3   Town and Country Planning, in the Ministry of Planning and Development, responsible for coastal development on the landward side of the coastal zone.

The confusion over management responsibility means that it is difficult to allocate resources to the responsible agency, and it is difficult to assign management, monitoring or enforcement responsibility to one agency. As a result, in several areas there is no single responsible agency for particular natural resources in Trinidad and Tobago, and there is frequent duplication of work.

Table 6.2 *Current gaps in environmental legislation in Trinidad and Tobago*

Gaps	Agency voicing concern	Scale of impact
New laws that demand public input into the development of new laws	National Parks Office, GOTT	Operational arrangements
Clarification of property rights	Department of Marine Resources & Fisheries, THA	Constitutional order
Means of offering legal support and protection for managers of natural resources	Environmental NGO	Organizational structures
Means of improving enforcement of existing laws	Workshop group-discussion outcome	Constitutional order
Means of legally protecting volunteer wardens, who could be activated through a co-management arrangement	Environmental NGO	Organizational structures

Note: GOTT = Government of Trinidad and Tobago; THA = Tobago House of Assembly
Source: Adapted from Tompkins and others (2002). Data derived from interviews and stakeholder workshop, October–November 1999

There is also a perception among resource managers that they have inadequate legal protection, and that there is inadequate enforcement of existing laws, and a lack of legal support for the agency enforcing the legislation or regulations. At present there is a lack of clear property rights for natural resources, especially coastal resources. Not only is there overlapping legislation that allocates property rights to different owners, but legislation intended to demarcate protected areas has, in some cases, been disputed with claims that the boundaries are inaccurately drawn. The outcome of inaccurate definitions is that property rights are unclear.

Designated MPAs are a pertinent example of unclear rights and responsibilities. The marine and coastal area of a site, including the reefs, the fish and other benthic life-forms, is the property of the state. Access permits are granted to fishermen to pass through it, although not to extract within the marine park. Reef tour operators and other boat tour or jet-ski operators also require licences to operate within the marine park. The diversity of functions and the range of property rights within the coastal zone in the Buccoo Reef area highlight the complexity of coastal zone management. In Trinidad and Tobago this complexity is exacerbated by the array of formal institutions engaged in managing coastal resources.

The necessary legal changes for successful, integrated and inclusive coastal zone management in Trinidad and Tobago as perceived by these diverse government agencies (see Table 6.2) are substantial, and may require more than just additional regulations being drafted. For example, as one individual noted, the problem of poor enforcement of laws is not just a problem for environmental management, but is a social problem that affects all areas of government in Trinidad and Tobago.

Table 6.3 *Organizational constraints to integrated and inclusive approaches*

Organizational areas	Perceived problems
Operational	Inadequate staff trained in integrated and inclusive approaches. Inadequate full-time outreach staff. Few successful examples of integrated and inclusive approaches. Overuse of external consultants.
Structural	Information hoarding. Inadequate public access to information. Project-driven approaches impose project cycle and timetabling. Government workers slow to adapt methods used by external groups and communities.

Source: Tompkins and others (2002). Data derived from interviews and stakeholder workshop, October–November 1999

Structurally, governments of small island states often suffer from a lack of specialist staff skills to implement integrated and inclusive approaches. Government staff inexperienced in developing integrated and inclusive approaches to projects may be unwilling to include unfamiliar integrated and inclusive techniques in project design. Insufficient full-time public outreach staff or community workers to engage stakeholders can be a major constraint. In many cases it is not just that the legislation and constitution are ambiguous. Government employees may hide behind old legislation to avoid working with stakeholders. And they are not trained in the newer, more inclusionary methods. This lack of training and field experience may both deter and disempower staff. There is limited information available to government staff on how to engage stakeholders, and there are few examples within government detailing successful inclusion of stakeholders. The cumulative effect of these structural issues is that staff in regulatory agencies often consider the inclusion of stakeholders as impractical for resource management.

The problems that can arise from inappropriate or unresponsive government structures are clear in Trinidad and Tobago. During a prioritization of major issues facing the tourism sector for the National Tourism Stakeholder Consultation in 1998, the institutional framework was singled out as the biggest problem facing the tourism sector in Tobago. Specifically, the issues of confusion over the roles of the different government agencies, lack of communication between institutions, lack of harmonization of laws, lack of clear guidelines for management, and no authority or responsibility assigned to some areas were highlighted as the most important issues.

The structure of the formal natural resource management institutions in Trinidad and Tobago imposes constraints on all arms of government (see Table 6.3). The lack of space for networks to develop is identified by many within the system as the bottleneck to the development of more integrated and inclusive approaches. But, in some cases, the constraints on the expansion of networks are self-imposed by the government agencies themselves. For example, government stakeholders suggested that if the government engaged in integrated and inclusive approaches, or co-management approaches to resource management, individual government agents may fear that they may appear unable to manage. New government agencies especially may need to develop public credibility to achieve success. Consequently, they may avoid untested methods or approaches. The problem of perceived power loss by government may diminish as more government departments start to see the potential benefits of engaging communities in making decisions about, and managing, natural resources.

In other cases there are few possibilities to expand institutional networks because of the peculiarities of institutional structures and operational arrangements. For example, many government agencies use a project cycle approach to allocate financial resources. As a result their work is often dominated by project proposal preparation, assessment and appraisal. Projects are assessed on the basis of the achievement of objectives in given timeframes, and it is on this basis that projects are compared and prioritized. If funding is allocated the project is expected to be run to schedule and to achieve its objectives. The project cycle approach is fully entrenched in the government system, but it might be one of the reasons for the slow uptake of integrated and inclusive approaches in Trinidad and Tobago. Project timetables are fixed in the project proposal, and funders generally require project managers to deliver outputs according to project timetables. Funding is continued on the successful completion of intermediate targets. If inadequate time is initially allocated to inclusionary processes, this might be a stumbling block to the achievement of project deadlines as inclusionary processes can be time-consuming and unpredictable in terms of the length of time they take to complete. It is therefore difficult to assess at the outset of a project how much time should be allowed for participation. Even if a period of time is allocated to engage stakeholders it may not be adequate, and if a project leader is determined to meet inflexible project deadlines it might not be possible to engage stakeholders fully. The project cycle therefore does not support social learning or adaptive approaches to coastal management.

The issues relating to the project cycle, including the use of consultants to complete projects, are perceived by respondents within Trinidad and Tobago agencies essentially to be a problem of democratic structures. To allocate scarce resources equitably and efficiently, a systematic programme for resource allocation needs to be used. The project cycle approach, together with the logical framework, does not have the flexibility (in terms of time and financial resources) that participatory techniques often require. Further problems associated with a reliance on external consultants include the perception of marginalization and exclusion by local stakeholders.

At the *operational level*, low levels of social capital and local networks as well as limited access to spaces of engagement constitute significant constraints to participation in natural resource decision-making. Constraints to participation can arise from the high costs of involvement in terms of time or money. Alternatively, poor interpersonal communication, aggressive behaviour or strained intra-community relations can all act as constraints to participation. Table 6.4 shows the perceptions of stakeholders in Trinidad and Tobago of the

Table 6.4 *Constraints on stakeholder participation*

Constraints on stakeholders	Effect on local-level networks	Effect on spaces of engagement and external networks
High financial cost of participation	Negative	No significant effect
High time cost of participation	Negative	No significant effect
Poor skills development of leaders	Negative	Negative
Poor communication within groups	Negative	Negative
Poor communication between groups	No significant effect	Negative
Existence of widespread personalized conflict	No significant effect	Negative
No formal channels of communication between groups	No significant effect	Negative

constraints on them becoming directly involved in integrated and inclusive processes. It shows that the constraints, such as the high opportunity cost of time and underdeveloped communication, are perceived only negatively in terms of the impacts on both internal and external networks.

Integrated and inclusive approaches are generally iterative and time-consuming. The stakeholders involved are often asked to commit a substantial amount of their time and sometimes their finances to supporting aspects of resource management. This can create the potential problem of non-representativeness through a self-selection process, whereby those people who have the time or resources to attend meetings and offer input may not reflect the opinions and attitudes of others in the community or group.

Equally important is the issue of skills development, especially in leadership qualities and relationship management both within and between communities. Poor communication within groups, or poor communication between stakeholder groups and government, are constraints on participation in resource management. In those stakeholder groups that are poorly organized, the inability to develop a coherent message and deliver it to the appropriate agency is akin to exclusion. There might be historical reasons why some groups do not work well together, although the reasons for this are not known.

In the case of Trinidad and Tobago, then, there are a range of regulatory, structural and behavioural gaps that need to be addressed to facilitate more integrated and inclusive resource management. These gaps have been highlighted by those directly engaged in integrated and inclusive resource management. A conclusion from the empirical analysis of Trinidad and Tobago institutions involved in coastal zone management is that at each institutional scale there must be careful consideration of the nature of existing spaces of engagement and spaces of dependence (see Tompkins and others, 2002). Where there is no potential to modify or adapt these spaces to include other stakeholders, vertically or horizontally, it seems unlikely that there can be successful integrated and inclusive resource management. Provision of enabling legislation is without doubt an important prerequisite, but it is not sufficient. In general, social and organizational networks are the key to decision-making for resource management. Without appropriate institutional structures, conservation and development remain mired in conflict. But we do not need to throw up our hands and say 'our institutions constrain us: where we stand depends on where we sit'. There are structured research techniques to enable us to paint a picture of networks and institutions. Such research can enable strategies to at least point in the direction of appropriate institutional reform.

CONCLUSIONS

Making decisions where there are multiple and conflicting objectives is part and parcel of coastal zone management. The difficulty in resolving these conflicts often leads to inaction by all concerned. Trade-off analysis and inclusion requires finding a means to analyse and manage the conflicts that are a central part of coastal zone management. The success of conflict management determines whether conflict will hinder or promote sustainable resource use. It is not only conflict management that is important: one must also create a platform for negotiating resource use and consensus-building. Trust-building, empowerment, knowledge sharing and deliberation underpin this objective.

In summary, embedding inclusive and integrated processes within institutional structures is an important step towards integrating conservation and development in the coastal zone. Stakeholder inclusion and a recognition and accommodation of institutional forms must be part of an overall management approach, not just an add-on.

Chapter 7

Integrating Conservation and Development

ACCEPTING COMPLEXITY

There is no blueprint for inclusive and supported decision-making for coastal management. The examples and methods described in this book point to some general patterns in making coastal management legitimate, effective and equitable. Clearly issues such as trust, sensitivity to the scale and dynamics of the ecological system, and flexibility in the management institutions, are important components. But simply recommending that coastal resources are treated as common property resources and that institutions are established to integrate all stakeholder views is not sufficient. Issues of power, questions of consensus and the cross-scale nature of institutions stand as warnings and limitations to the application of a blueprint for participatory or inclusive management.

In the preceding chapters we have outlined methods and examples to promote inclusive management. We call this set of techniques trade-off analysis (Brown and others, 2001b) and are applying this framework in a variety of resource management contexts, from forest management to climate change. In essence, the approach emphasizes both engagement with and analysis of the importance and influence of stakeholders in the management of coastal resources. Further, it suggests that envisioning future coastal states and exploring the values and priorities of stakeholders through deliberative processes enhance the potential for co-management. But a further necessary step is an understanding and accommodation of the heterogeneity of institutional form and context within which consensus about ways forward can emerge.

Thus, trade-off analysis is both a positive and constructive approach to management. In proposing such a set of tools and frameworks, there is always a danger of surprising and confounding factors. Indeed, the emerging science of adaptive management stresses the unexpected and ultimately unpredictable nature of the future, and of the evolution of natural systems (Kates and Clark, 1996; Gunderson, 2000). In addition, the uncritical adoption of participatory techniques and the application of essentially non-democratic means of resolving conservation and development dilemmas pose great challenges in this area. The whole edifice of co-management and inclusive decision-making for coastal areas can come crashing down when the foundations of legitimacy and trust are not in place. The pile-drivers of social capital and institution-forming need to be the first on-site for building sustainable co-management. Each of these issues is taken up in turn in this chapter as we seek a way forward for balancing conservation and development.

CRITIQUES OF PARTICIPATION

The move towards participatory management of coastal zones reflects wider social and policy changes. New institutional arrangements have in one sense extended the opportunities for citizens and resource users to become involved in issues that directly affect their well-being, their sense of place and their ownership of the future. But involvement has in effect been re-conceptualized on their behalf by the top–down imposition of these new institutional forms, which retain the right to specify who is involved and what their rights to be informed and consulted are. In every policy sphere affecting coastal zones, from World Bank lending criteria to the European Union's Environmental Action Plans, there is a belief in the increased effectiveness of decisions made through consultation or participation.

Yet the trend towards increased participation stems from the inability of many existing legitimate institutions to undertake coastal management. This inability is often a result of the retrenchment of local government and central government and a lack of resources to undertake effective management. At the same time as there are supposedly increased opportunities for participation, there are local, national and global resistance movements, shunning the new institutions of participation in favour of mass protest and direct action. These are manifest not just globally through protests against globalization, but in a myriad of campaigns against coastal degradation. They encompass consumer boycotts and campaigns in Europe against unsustainable fisheries exploitation from the fishing grounds of poor and fisheries-dependent countries. They also encompass social movements protesting against mangrove destruction in many coastal states in India. Thus the notions of integrating conservation with development must be cognisant of the wider, and in some cases global, political economy of the use of coastal resources and the new social movements and institutions outside the simple local consultation processes advocated as the new way in resource management.

Measures of success

Is participatory and inclusive management a success if agreed management practices lead to the deterioration of coastal ecosystems? This question encapsulates a number of dilemmas within the integrative, adaptive management paradigm. Who determines what is successful and whose values count? Is success defined in instrumental terms? Or is success defined in terms of empowerment and inclusion of the stakeholders? There have been valuable attempts to learn the lessons from deliberative processes, though they remain few and far between for integrated and inclusive coastal management processes. Although there are some difficulties in developing appropriate indicators for the success of inclusive processes, the fundamental choice of criteria is the most contested area.

Defining success revolves around whether success should be measured in terms of the process by which management practices develop, or the outcome, or both. Is a successful participatory project one where many people are engaged and stay engaged in the management process, or one where the management objectives are achieved? Should success be judged by the features of the management programme or by the outputs? Success appears to be essentially a subjective concept that can be assessed from many different viewpoints. The perceived success of a project may differ depending on the evaluator, whether he or she is a policy-maker, a local resource user or a researcher (Steins and Edwards, 1999).

The success of a participatory or inclusive approach has to be considered in the light of the objective for which the approach is applied. Participatory management approaches can be used to improve the quality of management by considering a range of views and opinions in the decision-making process. Alternatively, participation can be used to empower communities or groups and to build social capital. These two objectives are clearly fundamentally different and hence should not be judged on a single set of success criteria.

If, on the one hand, the objective of a participatory approach is utilitarian, namely to ensure that as wide a range of views and opinions as possible is considered in the decision-making process, then its success has to be judged on the ability to implement the final decision. A decision that is widely supported and provides the majority of stakeholders with an outcome that is acceptable could be considered a success. If the major objectives of participatory management are to empower excluded social groups and encourage social or political change, then other success criteria are required. In this case, participation is likely to offer an effective means of including and empowering stakeholders and building trust, although it may not generate the desired conservation or development objectives of an outside conservation group or institution. Participatory processes that are designed to bring about social change can be considered in terms of their ability to influence research, education and action. Each component of such a participatory process could be assessed by its generation of practical solutions to local community problems. The longer-term success of such an approach is then judged by its impact on changing the power relations within a community or society.

Participation in decision-making is clearly not a single panacea to coastal zone management, as the global experiences of participatory approaches reveal. In the Philippines, one estimate of the success rate of community-based coastal resource management projects suggests that one-half of all community-based projects fail to make any discernible difference to coastal resource use (Alcala, 1998). This is down to a number of factors, including the autonomy of coastal communities and economies: small communities, in particular, are often not able to protect their resources against strong external threats. In general, community participation for natural resource management is beset by a myriad of problems, and may not always be in the best interests of either the targeted community or the natural resource being managed (see Cooke and Kothari, 2001). Participation can contribute to empowerment and self-reliance, but these are not necessarily criteria for environmental health improvements. Indeed, empowering local communities to engage in coastal zone management is not guaranteed to lead to a sustainable project or outcome, or to enable that community to better define its property rights (Jorge, 1997).

Even with contested concepts of the success and objectives of inclusive management, there is empirical evidence that community involvement can create workable institutional arrangements for natural resource management in certain circumstances. Workable arrangements appear to have occurred when communities have greater interest and experience in the sustainable use of the resources than externally located managers (Brosius and others, 1998). This observation ties in with the wider experience of common property management outlined in Chapter 2 (see Agrawal, 2001). Where there has been extensive experience of discrete community-based management or participatory approaches, lessons on success are emerging.

In the USA, participatory environmental management has been popular in the states managing resources around the Great Lakes and across the USA–Canada border. In a review of that experience, Beierle and Konisky (2000) identify a range of management attributes that appeared to be important to the success of the participatory approach. Success, in this case, was defined in terms of the achievement of three goals: incorporation of public values into decision-making, resolving conflict among competing interests and restoring a degree of trust in public agencies. Where there were shared jurisdictions (either across international or state boundaries) there tended to be less successful participation. The USA experience suggests that participatory processes can be successful at developing supported environmental management strategies, though much depends on the flexibility and willingness to engage in and sustain the process by the decision-making regulatory agency.

In agreement with the USA evidence on determinants of success, we suggest that there are four attributes contributing to both the effectiveness and legitimizing objectives of participatory management. These are the quality of the deliberative process in terms of communication, consensus and fairness; the level of interaction and communication with the key decision-making agency; the level of commitment to the process by the key decision-making agency; and whether there were any shared management or planning jurisdictions. The first of these, the perception of fairness in the process, is the most fundamental.

In summary, the mixed results from examples of community participation in resource management and decision-making suggest that participatory approaches to resource management are constrained or promoted by the quality of the process as much as by the objectives, and by the institutional context as much as by the personalities involved. The institutional arrangements, the legislative framework and the organizational and technical skills of the communities determine success (Tompkins and others, 2002). But the definition of objectives and the definition of success are political and contested.

Power and representation

The issues around defining objectives and defining success come back to those of power. It is only when deliberative and inclusive decision-making moves away from consultation and towards sharing responsibility and changing the underlying property rights that power relations actually change. Simple consultation exercises, where data is extracted to facilitate further rigid coastal zone management, do not lead to legitimate or sustainable management. But as outlined in Chapter 6, deliberative processes are only one part of decision-making processes. Representative governments are, in effect, elected to implement a societal consensus about present modern dilemmas and to plan for the future. What, in those societies where there is a semblance of representative democracy, are the roles of potentially unrepresentative consultative arrangements for making decisions about local resources? These issues are, as O'Neill (2001) has argued, not about the empirics of deliberative institutions: how statistically representative can such fora be? Rather, representativeness is a normative issue about how inclusionary management reinforces the status quo in society and excludes some views. O'Neill (2001) articulates these normative issues as falling into two categories: 'unrepresentation for contingent reasons' and 'problems of the very possibility of representation'.

First, deliberative processes are inevitably biased in favour of the powerful. Underlying ability, willingness and capacity to be heard and to articulate preferences are unevenly distributed by class, age, gender and ethnicity. The participation of any group is contingent on the underlying social structures. Much empirical evidence suggests that the participants in many stakeholder groups tend to be those with the time or the money to participate (Forest, 1998). Second, many stakeholders will not participate in apparently technocratic resource management. As we saw earlier, those reluctant to participate may be precisely the stakeholders who would most benefit from both the outcomes of conservation and the empowerment of co-management. Participatory processes can only be transformative if they bring about a change in the underlying social order.

Other worldviews and perceptions defy inclusion in any deliberative or management process. Future generations and non-human beings pose particular problems of representation in decision-making processes (O'Neill, 2001). All decision-makers have an eye to the future and have some altruistic motives for conserving the environment for its intrinsic worth and for the enjoyment of future generations. Yet altruism and perceptions of nature and belief in its intrinsic right to exist are all unevenly distributed in society and remain fundamentally unrepresented in any meaningful way (Dryzek, 2000).

Third, it is clear that within participatory processes there are many potential problems that can arise from the interactions within a group. When dominated by risk-takers, a group can take more risky decisions than any of the individuals would take by themselves, and this can lead to a situation in which the group agrees on a course of action to which none of the individual members actually subscribe. Decision-making groups can be coerced by members within the group or by outsiders, and path-dependent 'groupthink', as psychologists have noted, can lead decisions in ways undesired by any stakeholder (Cooke, 2001). The impact of these problems will depend on the social and cultural setting, and the social capital through which individuals interact within society.

In Roatán in Honduras, a group of concerned citizens were drawn together to improve the management of a coastal area in which environmental quality was deteriorating. Without government support the social groups autonomously initiated a system of monitoring and management of their coastal resources. However, as Luttinger (1997) points out, while there was initial success based on building consensus among the stakeholders, the support of certain key stakeholders was lost when later conflicts arose that were not well managed. In particular, one key stakeholder withheld financial support that reduced the enforcement capability of the group, and this in turn led to a further loss of support by other stakeholders and the collapse of the participatory process. The exclusion of a key stakeholder is common in these situations (Hodgson, 1997). In the context of Honduras, the existence of social stratification by social class may be the cause of the inclusion of some groups, notably the social elite, and the exclusion of the non-elite (Forest, 1998). This social stratification and separation of classes has been overcome in some cases by the development of strong relationships and good communication between certain stakeholder groups. However, those groups with weak or non-existent relationships with other groups and poor ability to communicate tend to be excluded. Public participation in decision-making in the case of Roatán appears to have been limited to the social elite and those groups with good communication and networking skills.

Central to the issues of power and representation are knowledge and the control of knowledge. The positivist tradition in science has ensured that scientific knowledge, as generally defined, is the only legitimate form of knowledge. It excludes all others and is vested in the machinery of government and law. Such narrow faith in one reality has led to spectacular failures in high modernist projects, and to the spatial and social exclusion of other forms of knowledge (Scott, 1998). Incorporating the precautionary principle into everyday management, for example, is immensely difficult for traditional ecosystem management (O'Riordan, 2000). Yet such precautionary and stewardship action is central to many forms of traditional resource management. Traditional knowledge in this sense does not mean 'coming from some time in the past'. Rather, it means knowledge that is held in different forms (collectively or orally), develops through different learning systems and evolves over time with changing ecological realities (see Berkes and others, 1998; 2000). In the tradition of modern science, stakeholder discourse and traditional or 'local' knowledge are not recognized as valid (Selener, 1997). Inclusionary and deliberative processes provide an opportunity to include alternative forms of knowledge in the decision-making process. Opening up the concept of knowledge to include individual and group preferences ensures that both the scientific and the constructed have their place.

An important component of inclusion and deliberation is the role of social learning and the understanding of science and of other stakeholders' perceptions. A range of meanings of 'social learning' exist, but in very general terms, social learning either refers to learning by individuals in social settings through social conditioning, or learning by groups or organizations through interaction (Parson and Clark, 1995). It has been suggested that knowledge is created through the interaction of people with the physical environment (Dewey, 1930). Knowledge is reflexive and evolves as individuals reapply it to determine its validity, thereby creating 'learning by doing'. By disseminating scientific information and information about different perceptions and preferences, communities and groups can learn through their interaction with the information and views of others.

Learning through discussion also engages people in decision-making and helps determine local needs and priorities (Hailey, 2001). It can also generate stakeholder momentum to move from management planning to implementation (Olsen, 1993). Social learning has been proposed as an important element in decision-making, as it is a means of evolving and improving the collective understanding of complex environmental problems (Tonn and others, 2000). Social learning processes not only relate to stakeholder learning about the science of resource use and management, but also concern the respective roles of science and local knowledge in resource management. Engaging stakeholders in deliberative and inclusionary social learning processes builds relationships among stakeholders based on similar moral, social or cultural values. Such relationships can lead to the development of social networks that can provide support to management.

Inclusive, learning-based processes that facilitate deliberation and participation cannot, however, guarantee transparent, effective and supported decision-making. Environmental decision-making is often messy and contingent upon the intermingling of power, interests and chance (Parson and Clark, 1995). Nevertheless, the provision of an opportunity for social learning gives people the time and space they may need to consider methods for management and their own understanding of the opportunities that exist for alternative approaches.

In summary, the challenges involved in bringing different worldviews and immediate economic interests into coastal management include those of measuring success, representation and power, and the recognition of diverse ways of knowing the world. Deliberative processes are only likely to reinforce the status quo in social relations in a community. So the definition of what is successful remains problematic. As we know, history is usually written by the winners.

WHAT WE MEAN BY INTEGRATED AND INCLUSIVE MANAGEMENT

In this book we suggest that co-management arrangements are most likely to evolve where there has been effective participation in decision-making (see also White and others, 1994; Berkes and others, 2001; Brown, 2002). This means the

---

BOX 7.1 LESSONS LEARNED: PRE-REQUISITES FOR INTEGRATING CONSERVATION AND DEVELOPMENT

Scoping the stakeholders and their interests

Homogenous stakeholder groups with clearly defined interests do not exist. Thorough stakeholder analyses are central to understanding the levels of support for decisions.

Understanding conflicts

There will always be conflicting stakeholders in multiple-use resources. Conflict management is a critical element of inclusive management and institutions.

Trust

Trust is a prerequisite. This means trust by all major interests in the decision-making processes, in the institutions and individuals making and implementing decisions, and in the institutions that define and enforce the laws.

Transparency of process

Co-management and consultative processes, and the channels of information and command, have to be understood by all the groups concerned. This is often a costly and resource-intensive aspect of inclusionary management, overlooked in resource planning.

Appropriate institutional forms

Formal and informal institutions can be defined by their constitutional and regulatory forms, organizational structures and social rules and norms of behaviour. All three elements must support integrated approaches.

Sharing and legitimizing knowledge

There is great diversity of ways of knowing the coastal zone. Traditional scientific knowledge and widely different worldviews and values exist. Decision-support tools must be able to manage all forms of information.

Sensitivity to the dynamics of ecosystems

Ultimately, human understanding of coastal processes and the impacts of management interventions is limited. Greater awareness and information from inclusive management and institutions can be used to promote institutional as well as ecosystem resilience.

---

early involvement of stakeholders in decision-making, representative participants and an independent and unbiased process of participation. In addition, effective participation is most likely where the outcomes of the participation have a perceptible and positive impact on decision-making (Rowe and Frewer, 2000). These conditions, coupled with the importance of open channels of communication and spaces for public deliberation, suggest the need for platforms and spaces where complex coastal zone management issues can be negotiated. Röling and Wagemakers (1998) and others suggest that platforms for collective action may be created when three conditions arise: when multiple stakeholders realize that they have the same interests; when the stakeholders have the influence to change one or more parts of the problem; and when the stakeholders are willing to work together to solve the problem.

In the light of these findings, we argue that the concept of integrated coastal zone management should be expanded to be more inclusionary and to engage deliberative processes. We have learned from our experience of developing tools and frameworks for integrating conservation and development and from researching the institutional determinants of the adoption of these practices. Some of these lessons are summarized in Box 7.1. Inclusion and deliberation should facilitate stakeholder understanding of the conflicts that exist, whether they are conflicts of interest, conflicts related to the lack of information or a lack of understanding of the information. Deliberative and inclusionary processes can also potentially provide the time and space for stakeholder learning and participation in decision-making. Such processes facilitate communication, which can build trust and harmonize stakeholder knowledge about resource management. In addition, inclusion and deliberation can lead to the evolution of a platform for collective action that offers the possibility for alternative institutions for coastal zone management, such as co-management arrangements.

This book reinforces the notion that the collaborative management of coastal zones has to be underpinned by several conditions. First, there must be an understanding of the stakeholders' interests and the use conflicts that exist at different scales. These conflicts could range from on-site conflicts between users, such as fishers and tourist industry workers, to national-level conflicts among land use planners and marine resource managers. Without careful analysis, key stakeholders can be excluded, creating an unrepresentative forum for deliberation and negotiation. Second, adequate time should be factored into planning processes to ensure that the stakeholders at all scales have the time to develop relationships of trust that enable them to deliberate together, to learn and to participate actively in management. The engagement and deliberation process could last for months or even years and will be successful if it is ultimately self-sustaining. The length of time depends on the nature and severity of the conflict and the number of stakeholders. Third, channels of communication have to be open to ensure that both verbal and non-verbal communication can occur. This communication may be about scientific information or about individual or group behaviour. Two-way open communication reduces mistrust, increases accessibility to information and builds networks of exchange. Where previous management approaches have led to a loss of trust, this is particularly important. Finally, through these processes a platform for collective action could be established. The creation of such a forum may facilitate the development of a collaborative management approach.

COASTS OF THE FUTURE

What do the tools and lessons for management in this book mean for the development of approaches to coastal zone management? The key issues are vertical and horizontal linkages towards the integration of management. This apparently technocratic improvement can only be realized when all parties are engaged in a discourse of the future, when the trade-offs between competing interests are made explicit, and when the institutions reflect the dynamism and complexity of the ecological systems of the coast. As we have seen throughout this book, coastal management in both its physical and social manifestations will always throw up surprises and hence requires flexibility, learning by doing and the comprehension of alternative values and knowledge.

Variability in ecological systems is in some ways inherently predictable, but in other ways is always surprising. Holling's (1986; 1995) 'theory of surprise' is based on the notion of discontinuities and on the nature of ecological systems. The philosophical basis of environmental management, he argues, is determined by the worldviews of nature where people managing resources conceive of the environment as either benign, balanced or resilient and able to reorganize itself. Whichever view is adopted of how ecological systems work, surprises are inherent in the system. It is human intervention, more often than not, that leads to surprises that confound social expectations. Sometimes these surprises are unpredictable from a scientific viewpoint. Sometimes they are predictable with hindsight. These surprises are more often than not unpleasant ones, generally harmful to social resilience and human welfare. But they may also create windows of opportunity in environmental management (Kates and Clark, 1996).

The world's coastal zones are critical resources in the necessary transition to sustainability required in the upcoming century. This is particularly so because of the trends outlined in Chapter 1: the world's populations are increasingly drawn to coastal zones; the globalization of the world economy exacerbates trends of overexploitation and degradation, and economic and social globalization is reducing the geographical, spatial and temporal factors constraining development and utilization of natural resources. Thus the conservation of ecosystems, traditional societies and ways of life, and a secure environment for living space and recreation are under threat. In this book we have given much space to the lessons from Trinidad and Tobago in the West Indies. There, tourism development continues apace, perhaps with a greater recognition of the need for autonomy in Tobago within the twin-island national governing structures, and for the autonomy of local stakeholders to have their voice heard in decisions that affect the long-term resilience of themselves and the reefs of Tobago. In East Anglia, the long-term future of Seahenge is still in doubt. The protagonists in the debate over its future call for a public inquiry, the traditional form of public consultation on such issues in the UK. But perhaps the widely divergent values and beliefs of how cultural heritage should be treated and how the dynamism of the sea should be respected mean that noone will ever be satisfied with compromise.

As this book has pointed out, the conservation of coastal resources and their sustainable development is mediated through institutions, legal systems of property rights and access to the resources by diverse users who have multiple and conflicting interests. Thus it is institutions, whether clarified in law or customary rights, that constitute how human interaction with coastal resources actually take place. It is the rights of fishers to harvest, the rights of industrial plants to discharge pollutants, the rights of government agencies to exclude users from a marine park that in effect determine the direction, rate and scope of environmental change in coastal areas. To steer institutions towards sustainability requires trust, cooperation and respect for diverse rights and ways of knowing and engaging with the world.

Further Reading

Coastal zone management

Kay, R and Alder, J (1998) *Coastal Planning and Management*, Spon, London

Cicin-Sain, B and Knecht, R W (1998) *Integrated Coastal and Ocean Management: Concepts and Experiences*, Island Press, Washington, DC

Gustavson, K, Huber, R M and Ruitenbeek, J (eds) (2000) *Integrated Coastal Zone Management of Coral Reefs: Decision Support Modeling*, World Bank, Washington, DC

von Bodungen, B and Turner, R K (eds) (2001) *Science and Integrated Coastal Management*, Dahlam Workshop Report 85, Dahlem University Press, Berlin

Integrated Coastal Zone Management is a journal and internet site that provides topical and accessible articles on coastal management and links to international conventions that apply to coastal zones. Available at www.porttechnology.org/iczm. Other relevant academic journals include *Ocean and Coastal Management* (published by Elsevier, www.elsevier.nl) and *Coastal Management* (published by Routledge, www.routledge.com).

The USA Office of Ocean and Coastal Resource Management web site focuses mainly on the USA but also provides generic information. There is much about the US coastal zone management programme, including a copy of the US Coastal Zone Management Act. Available at www.ocrm.nos.noaa.gov/czm.

Community-based natural resource and adaptive management

McShane, T and Wells, M (eds) (forthcoming, 2003) *Integrated Conservation and Development Practice: Current State and Directions for the Future*, Columbia University Press, New York

Western, D, Wright, R M and Strum, S C (eds) (1994) *Natural Connections: Perspectives in Community-based Conservation*, Island Press, Washington, DC

Salafsky, N, Maroluis, R and Redford, K (2001) *Adaptive Management: A Tool for Conservation Practitioners*, Biodiversity Support Program, Washington, DC. Available on-line at www.BSPonline.org

Ghimere, K and Pimbert, M P (eds) (1997) *Social Change and Conservation*, Earthscan, London

IDS Bulletin (1997) Special issue on Community-based Sustainable Development, vol 28 no 4

Hulme, D and Murphree, M (eds) (2001) *African Wildlife and Livelihoods: The Promise and Performance of Community Conservation*, James Currey, Oxford

McCay, B J and Acheson, J M (eds) (1987) *The Question of the Commons: The Culture and Ecology of Communal Resources*, University of Arizona Press, Tuscon

Conservation Ecology is an on-line journal focusing on the ecological basis for conservation and adaptive management as well as economics, and the social sciences concerned with conservation and sustainable development. Available at www.consecol.org.

The manual *Trade-off Analysis for Participatory Coastal Zone Decision Making* provides specific guidance on how to carry out the trade-off analysis approach outlined in this book. Practical examples are given of stakeholder analysis, multi-criteria analysis and consensus-building techniques. Available at www.uea.ac.uk/dev/publink/resmgt.shtml.

CIFOR, the Centre for International Forestry Research, has a research programme on Adaptive Co-management in Forests. Many papers, including a manual on the application of multi-criteria analysis to sustainable forest management, are available through their web site at www.cifor.cgiar.org/acm.

Coral reefs, ecosystem services and environmental change

Birkeland, C (eds) (1997) *Life and Death of Coral Reefs*, Chapman and Hall, New York
White, A T, Hale, L Z, Renard, Y and Cortesi, L (1994) *Collaborative and Community-based Management of Coral Reefs: Lessons from Experience*, Kumarian Press, Hartford
Ecological Economics (1999) Special issue on The Ecology of Ecosystem Services, vol 29 no 2 (published by Elsevier www.elsevier.nl)

ReefBase is a global information system on coral reefs. ReefBase provides access to data and information on coral reefs and associated shallow tropical habitats. Available at www.reefbase.org.

The UNEP World Conservation Monitoring Centre (WCMC) provides information services on conservation and on the world's living resources. The data provided include summary tables of marine statistics and maps showing coral reefs and mangroves from a number of countries, generated from the global reef database. Available at www.wcmc.org.uk/marine.

Land–Ocean Interactions in the Coastal Zone (LOICZ) is an international science project within the IGBP effort to understand the Earth system. LOICZ is attempting to determine the nature of dynamic interaction in the coastal zone at regional and global scales and the role of coasts in the global environment, and to assess how future changes in these areas will affect their use by people. It also attempts to provide a sound scientific basis for the future integrated management of coastal areas on a sustainable basis. Its web site (www.nioz.nl/loicz) provides information about datasets on coastal typologies, coastal change, coastal sediment, carbon and other processes.

Coral Reefs is the journal of the International Society for Reef Studies (published by Springer, www.springer-ny.com). Topics covered include population dynamics and community ecology of reef organisms, energy and nutrient flows, biogeochemical cycles, reef response to natural and anthropogenic stress, behavioural ecology, sedimentology, evolutionary ecology of the reef biota and the science that underpins reef management.

Fisheries, ocean governance and ocean law

Pinkerton, E W and Weinstein, M (1995) *Fisheries That Work: Sustainability Through Community Based Management*, David Suzuki Foundation, Vancouver
Acheson, J M (1988) *The Lobster Gangs of Maine*, University Press of New England, Hanover

Pomeroy, R S (ed) (1994) *Community Management and Common Property of Coastal Fisheries in Asia and the Pacific: Concepts, Methods and Experiences*, International Centre for Living and Aquatic Resources Management, Manila

Berkes, F, Mahon, R, McConney, P, Pollnac, R and Pomeroy, R (2001) *Managing Small-scale Fisheries. Alternative Directions and Methods,* IDRC, Ottawa

This book looks beyond the scope of conventional fishery management to alternative concepts, tools, methods and conservation strategies. Available at www.idrc.ca/acb/.

Polunin, N V C and Roberts, C M (eds) (1996) *Reef Fisheries*, Chapman and Hall, London

Ecological Economics (1999) Special issue on Ecological Economics and Sustainable Governance of the Ocean, vol 31 no 2 (published by Elsevier, www.elsevier.nl)

The United Nations Convention on the Law of the Sea (UNCLOS) lays down a comprehensive regime of law and order in the world's oceans and seas, establishing rules governing all uses of the oceans and their resources. Information on the status and texts of UNCLOS are available at www.un.org/Depts/los. Information on further UN activity in the area is available at www.unac.org/monitor/SusDev/issues/oceans.html.

The Food and Agriculture Organization of the UN also provides much information on fisheries production and status through its Fisheries Department. Available at www.fao.org.

References

Adger, W N (2000) 'Social and ecological resilience: are they related?' *Progress in Human Geography*, vol 24, pp347–364

Adger, W N (2002) 'Governing natural resources: institutional adaptation and resilience' in Berkhout, F, Leach, M and Scoones, I (eds) *Negotiating Environmental Change: Advances in Environmental Social Science*, Edward Elgar, Cheltenham

Adger, W N and Brooks, N (in press, 2002) 'Does global environmental change cause natural disasters?' in Pelling, M (ed) *Natural Disasters in a Globalising World*, Routledge, London

Adger, W N and Luttrell, C (2000) 'Property rights and the utilisation of wetlands', *Ecological Economics*, vol 35, pp75–89

Agrawal, A (2001) 'Common property institutions and sustainable governance of resources', *World Development*, vol 29, pp1649–1672

Agrawal, A and Gibson, C C (1999) 'Enchantment and disenchantment: the role of community in natural resource conservation', *World Development*, vol 27, pp629–649

Alcala, A C (1998) 'Community-based coastal resource management in the Philippines: a case study', *Ocean and Coastal Management*, vol 38, pp179–186

Alder, J (1996) 'Have tropical marine protected areas worked? An initial analysis of their success', *Coastal Management*, vol 24, pp97–114

Allison, E H (2001) 'Big laws, small catches: global ocean governance and the fisheries crisis', *Journal of International Development*, vol 13, pp933–950

Andersson, J and Ngazi, Z (1998) 'Coastal communities' production choices, risk diversification, and subsistence behaviour: responses in periods of transition', *Ambio*, vol 27, pp686–693

Arrow, K J (1951) *Social Choice and Individual Values*, Yale University Press, New Haven, CT

Baland, J M and Platteau, J P (1996) *Halting Degradation of Natural Resources: Is There a Role for Rural Communities?*, Clarendon, Oxford

Barbier, E (1993) 'Sustainable use of wetlands valuing tropical wetland benefits: economic methodologies and applications', *Geographical Journal*, vol 159, pp22–32

Baron, J (1997) 'Biases in the quantitative measurement of values in public decisions', *Psychological Bulletin*, vol 122, pp72–88

Bateman, I and Willis, K (eds) (1999) *Valuing Environmental Preference: Theory and Practice of the Contingent Valuation Method in the US, EU and Developing Countries*, Oxford University Press, Oxford

Beierle, T C and Konisky, D M (2000) 'Values, conflict, and trust in participatory environmental planning', *Journal of Policy Analysis and Management*, vol 19, pp587–602

Bell, F and Leeworthy, V (1990) 'Recreational demand by tourists for saltwater beach days', *Journal of Environmental Economics and Management*, vol 18, pp189–205

Berg, H, Ohman, M C, Troeng, S and Linden, O (1998) 'Environmental economics of coral reef destruction in Sri Lanka', *Ambio*, vol 27, pp627–634

Berkes, F (ed) (1989) *Common Property Resources: Ecology and Community-based Sustainable Development*, Belhaven, London

Berkes, F, Colding, J and Folke, C (2000) 'Rediscovery of traditional ecological knowledge as adaptive management', *Ecological Applications*, vol 10, pp1251–1262

Berkes, F and Folke, C (eds) (1998) *Linking Social and Ecological Systems: Management Practices and Social Mechanisms for Building Resilience*, Cambridge University Press, Cambridge

Berkes, F, Kislalioglu, M, Folke, C and Gadgil, M (1998) 'Exploring the basic ecological unit: ecosystem-like concepts in traditional societies', *Ecosystems*, vol 1, pp409–415

Berkes, F, Mahon, R, McConney, P, Pollnac, R C and Pomeroy, R S (2001) *Managing Small-Scale Fisheries: Alternative Directions and Methods*, International Development Research Centre, Ottawa

Bernard, H R (1994) *Research Methods in Anthropology: Qualitative and Quantitative Approaches,* second edition, Sage, Thousand Oaks, CA

Birnie, P W and Boyle, A E (1992) *International Law and the Environment*, Clarendon, Oxford

Blumenthal, D and Jannick, J L (2000) 'A classification of collaborative management methods', *Conservation Ecology* vol 4, no 2, article 13, available at www.consecol.org/Journal/vol4/iss2/

Bockstael, N, Costanza, R, Strand, I, Boynton, W, Bell, K and Waigner, L (1995) 'Ecological economic modelling and valuation of ecosystems', *Ecological Economics*, vol 14, pp143–159

Boersma, P D and Parrish, J K (1999) 'Limiting abuse: marine protected areas, a limited solution', *Ecological Economics*, vol 31, pp287–304

Boyer, D, Cole, J and Batholomae, C (2000) 'Southwestern Africa: Northern Benguela Current region', *Marine Pollution Bulletin*, vol 41, pp123–140

Briguglio, L (1995) 'Small island developing states and their economic vulnerabilities', *World Development*, vol 23, pp1615–1632

Bromley, D W (1998) 'Searching for sustainability: the poverty of spontaneous order', *Ecological Economics*, vol 24, pp231–240

Brosius, J P, Tsing, A L and Zerner, C (1998) 'Representing communities: histories and politics of community-based natural resource management', *Society and Natural Resources*, vol 11, pp157–168

Brown, B E, Dunne, R P, Goodson, M S and Douglas A E, (2000) 'Bleaching patterns in reef corals', *Nature*, vol 404, pp142–143

Brown, K (2002) 'Innovations in conservation and development', *Geographical Journal*, vol 168, pp6–17

Brown, K, Turner, R K, Hameed, H and Bateman, I (1997) 'Environmental carrying capacity and tourism development in the Maldives and Nepal', *Environmental Conservation*, vol 24, pp316–325

Brown, K, Adger, W N, Tompkins, E L, Bacon, P, Shim, D and Young, K (1999) *Evaluating Trade-Offs Between Users of Marine Protected Areas in the Caribbean*, Final Technical Report to DFID Natural Resources Systems Programme, Overseas Development Group, School of Development Studies, University of East Anglia, Norwich

Brown, K and Rosendo, S (2000) 'The institutional architecture of extractive reserves in Rondonia, Brazil', *Geographical Journal*, vol 166, pp35–48

Brown, K, Adger, W N and Tompkins, E (2001a) *Building Consensus Among Stakeholders for Management of Natural Resources at the Land–Water Interface*, Report to Natural Resources Systems Programme, UK Department for International Development, Overseas Development Group, University of East Anglia, Norwich

Brown, K, Adger, W N, Tompkins, E, Bacon, P, Shim, D and Young, K (2001b) 'Trade-off analysis for marine protected area management', *Ecological Economics*, vol 37, pp417–434

Brown, V, Smith, D I, Wiseman, R and Handmer, J (1995) *Risks and Opportunities: Managing Environmental Conflict and Change*, Earthscan, London

Buck, S J (1989) 'Multi-jurisdictional resources: testing a typology for problem structuring' in Berkes, F (ed) *Common Property Resources: Ecology and Community-based Sustainable Development*, Belhaven, London

Butler, R W (1980) 'The concept of a tourist area cycle of evolution: implications for management of resources', *Canadian Geographer*, vol 24, pp5–16

Carter, T R and La Rovere, E L (2001) 'Developing and applying scenario' in McCarthy, J J, Canziani, O, Leary, N A, Dokken, D J and White, K S (eds) *Climate Change 2001: Impacts, Adaptation and Vulnerability. IPCC Working Group II*, Cambridge University Press, Cambridge

Chesson, J, Clayton, H and Whitworth, B (1999) 'Evaluation of fisheries management systems with respect to sustainable development', *ICES Journal of Marine Science*, vol 56, pp980–984

Cicin-Sain, B (1993) 'Sustainable development and integrated coastal management', *Ocean and Coastal Management*, vol 21, pp11–43

Clague, C (1997) 'The new institutional economics and economic development' in Clague, C (ed) *Institutions and Economic Development: Growth and Governance in Less Developed and Post-Socialist Countries*, Johns Hopkins University Press, Baltimore

Clark, J R (1996) *Coastal Zone Management Handbook*, Lewis Publishers, Boca Raton, FL

Collins, A (1999) 'Tourism development and natural capital', *Annals of Tourism Research*, vol 26, pp98–109

Cooke, B (2001) 'The social psychological limits of participation' in Cooke, B and Kothari, U (eds) *Participation: The New Tyranny?* Zed Books, London

Cooke, B and Kothari, U (eds) (2001) *Participation: The New Tyranny?* Zed Books, London

Coppin, A and Olsen, R N (1998) ' Earnings and ethnicity in Trinidad and Tobago', *Journal of Development Studies*, vol 34, no 3, pp116–134

Cortes, J and Risk, M J (1985) 'A reef under siltation stress, Cahuita, Costa Rica', *Bulletin of Marine Science*, vol 36, pp339–356

Costanza, R, d'Arge, R, de Groot, R, Farber, S, Grasso, M, Hannon, B, Limburg, K, Naeem, S, O'Neill, R V, Paruelo, J, Raskin, R G, Sutton, P and van den Belt, M (1997) 'The value of the world's ecosystem services and natural capital', *Nature*, vol 387, pp253–260

Costanza, R, d'Arge, R, de Groot, R, Farber, S, Grasso, M, Hannon, B, Limburg, K, Naeem, S, O'Neill, R V, Paruelo, J, Raskin, R G, Sutton, P and van den Belt, M (1998) 'The value of ecosystem services: putting the issues in perspective', *Ecological Economics*, vol 25, pp67–72

Costanza, R, Kemp, M and Boynton, W (1995) 'Scale and biodiversity in estuarine ecosystems' in Perrings, C, Maler, K G, Folke, C, Holling, C S and Jansson, B O (eds) *Biodiversity Loss: Economic and Ecological Issues*, Cambridge University Press, Cambridge

Cox, K R (1998) 'Spaces of dependence, spaces of engagement and the politics of scale, or: looking for local politics', *Political Geography*, vol 17, pp1–23

Crance, C and Draper, D (1996) 'Socially co-operative choices: an approach to achieving resource sustainability in the coastal zone', *Environmental Management*, vol 20, pp175–184

Crooks, S and Turner, R K (1999) 'Integrated coastal management: sustaining estuarine natural resources', *Advances in Ecological Research*, vol 29, 241–289

Daily, G C (ed) (1997) *Nature's Services: Societal Dependence on Natural Ecosystems*, Island Press, Washington, DC

Davos, C A (1998) 'Sustaining co-operation for coastal sustainability', *Journal of Environmental Management*, vol 52, pp379–387

De Alberquerque, K and McElroy, J L (1992) 'Caribbean small-island tourism styles and sustainable strategies', *Environmental Management*, vol 16, pp619–632

Dewey, J (1930) *Human Nature and Conduct*, Henry Holt, New York

Dixon, J A, Fallon Scura, L and van't Hof, T (1993) 'Meeting ecological and economic goals: marine parks in the Caribbean', *Ambio*, vol 22, pp117–125

Done, T J (1999) 'Coral community adaptability to environmental change at the scales of regions, reefs and reef zones', *American Zoologist*, vol 39, pp66–79

Dorow, W (1981) 'Values and conflict behaviour: an exploration of conceptual relationships' in Dlugos, G and Weiermair, K (eds) *Management Under Differing Value Systems: Political, Social and Economical Perspectives in a Changing World*, Walter de Gruyter, Berlin

Dryzek, J S (1997) *The Politics of the Earth: Environmental Discourses*, Oxford University Press, Oxford

Dryzek, J S (2000) *Deliberative Democracy and Beyond: Liberals, Critics, Contestations*, Oxford University Press, Oxford

Dubinsky, Z and Stambler, N (1996) 'Marine pollution and coral reefs', *Global Change Biology*, vol 2, pp511–526

Edwards, V M and Steins, N A (1998) 'Developing an analytical framework for multiple-use commons', *Journal of Theoretical Politics*, vol 10, pp347–383

Evans, P (1996) 'Government action, social capital and development: reviewing the evidence on synergy', *World Development*, vol 24, pp1119–1132

FAO (2000) Data on world fisheries, FAO, Rome at www.fao.org

Fernandes, L, Ridgely, M A and van't Hof, T (1999) 'Multiple-criteria analysis integrates economic, ecological and social objectives for coral reef managers', *Coral Reefs*, vol 18, pp393–402

Few, R (2001) 'Containment and counter-containment: planner/community relations in conservation planning', *Geographical Journal*, vol 167, pp111–124

Fisher, R and Ury, W (1982) *Getting to Yes: Negotiating Agreement Without Giving In*, Hutchinson Press, London

Forest, N B (1998) 'Assessment of coastal regulations and implementation: case study of Roatan, Bay Islands, Honduras', *Coastal Management*, vol 26, pp125–155

Forester, J (1999) *The Deliberative Practitioner: Encouraging Participatory Planning Processes*, MIT Press, Cambridge

Geoghegan, T, Renard, Y, Brown, N and Krishnarayan, V (1999) *Evaluation of Caribbean Experiences in Participatory Planning and Management of Marine and Coastal Resources*, Technical Report 259, Caribbean Natural Resources Institute, Vieux Fort, St Lucia

Georgiou, S, Bateman, I J, Langford, I H and Day, R J (2000) 'Coastal bathing water health risks: developing means of assessing the adequacy of proposals to amend the 1976 EC Directive', *Risk Decision and Policy*, vol 5, pp49–68

Gezon, L (1997) 'Institutional structure and the effectiveness of integrated conservation and development projects: case study from Madagascar', *Human Organization*, vol 56, pp462–470

Giddens, A (1998) *The Third Way: The Renewal of Social Democracy*, Polity Press, Cambridge

Goodwin, P and Wright, G (1991) *Decision Analysis for Management Judgement*, John Wiley, Chichester

Gregory, R and Keeney, R L (1994) 'Creating policy alternatives using stakeholder values', *Management Science*, vol 40, pp1035–1048

Gregory, R and Slovic, P (1997) 'A constructive approach to environmental valuation', *Ecological Economics*, vol 21, pp175–181

Grimble, R J, Aglionby, J and Quan, J (1994) *Tree Resources and Environmental Policy: A Stakeholder Approach*, Socio-economic Series 7, Natural Resources Institute, Chatham

Grumbine, R E (1994) 'What is ecosystem management?' *Conservation Biology*, vol 8, pp27–38

Guitouni, A and Martel, J-M (1998) 'Tentative guidelines to help choosing an appropriate multi-criteria decision analysis method', *European Journal of Operational Research*, vol 109, pp501–521

Gunderson, L H (2000) 'Ecological resilience: in theory and application', *Annual Review of Ecology and Systematics*, vol 31, pp425–439

Gunderson, L H, Holling, C S and Light, S S (eds) (1995) *Barriers and Bridges to the Renewal of Ecosystems and Institutions*, Columbia University Press, New York

Gurocak, E R and Whittlesey, N K (1998) 'Multiple-criteria decision making: a case study of the Columbia River salmon recovery plan', *Environmental and Resource Economics*, vol 12, pp479–495

Hailey, J (2001) 'Beyond the formulaic: process and practice in South Asian NGOs' in Cooke, B and Kothari, U (eds) *Participation: The New Tyranny?*, Zed Books, London

Harriss, B (1992) 'Talking to traders about trade' in Devereux, S and Hoddinott, J (eds) *Fieldwork in Developing Countries*, Harvester Wheatsheaf, London

Hayward, B M (1995) 'The greening of participatory democracy: reconsideration of theory', *Environmental Politics*, vol 4, pp215–236

Hobbs, B, Changkong, V, Hamadeh, W and Stakhiv, E (1992) 'Does choice of multicriteria method matter? An experiment in water resources planning', *Water Resources Research*, vol 28, pp1767–1779

Hodgson, G (1997) 'Resource use: conflicts and management solutions' in Birkeland, C (eds) *Life and Death of Coral Reefs*, Chapman and Hall, New York

Hoegh-Guldberg, O (1999) 'Climate change, coral bleaching and the future of the world's coral reefs', *Marine and Freshwater Research*, vol 50, pp839–866

Holling, C S (1986) 'The resilience of terrestrial ecosystems: local surprise and global change' in Clark, W C and Munn, R E (eds) *Sustainable Development of the Biosphere*, Cambridge University Press, Cambridge

Holling, C S (1995) 'What barriers? What bridges?' in Gunderson, L, Holling, C S and Light, S S (eds) *Barriers and Bridges to the Renewal of Ecosystems and Institutions*, Columbia University Press, New York

Holmes, T and Scoones, I (2000) *Participatory Environmental Policy Processes: Experiences from North and South*, IDS Working Paper 113, Institute of Development Studies, University of Sussex, Brighton

Holmlund, C M and Hammer, M (1999) 'Ecosystem services generated by fish populations', *Ecological Economics*, vol 29, pp253–268

Howarth, R W, Billen, G, Swaney, D, Townsend, A, Jaworski, N, Lajtha, K, Downing, J A, Elmgren, R, Caraco, N, Jordan, T, Berendse, F, Freney, J, Kudeyarov, V, Murdoch, P and Zhao-Liang, Z (1996) 'Regional nitrogen budgets and riverine N and P fluxes for tje drainages to the North Atlantic Ocean: natural and human influences', *Biogeochemistry*, vol 35, pp75–139

Hughey, K F D, Cullen, R and Kerr, G N (2000) 'Stakeholder groups in fisheries management', *Marine Policy* vol 24, pp119–127.

Hunter, C J and Evans, C W (1995) 'Coral reefs in Kaneohe Bay, Hawaii: two centuries of western influence and two decades of data', *Bulletin of Marine Sciences*, vol 57, pp501–515

Hwang, C-L and Yoon, K (1981) *Multiple Attribute Decision Making, Methods and Applications: A State of the Art Survey*, Springer Verlag, Berlin

Imperial, M (1999) 'Institutional analysis and ecosystem-based management: the institutional analysis and development framework', *Environmental Management*, vol 24, pp449–465

Jackson, J B C, Kirby, M X, Berger, W H, Bjorndal, K A, Botsford, L W, Bourque, B J, Bradbury, R H, Cooke, R, Erlandson, J, Estes, J A, Hughes, T P, Kidwell, S, Lange, C B, Lenihan, H S, Pandolfi, J M, Peterson, C H, Steneck, R S, Tegner, M J and Warner, R R (2001) 'Historical overfishing and the recent collapse of coastal ecosystems', *Science*, vol 293, pp629–638

Janssen, R (1994) *Multiobjective Decision Support for Environmental Management*, Kluwer, Dordrecht

Jentoft, S (1989) 'Fisheries co-management: delegating government responsibility to fishermen's organisations', *Marine Policy*, vol 13, pp137–154

Jorge, M A (1997) 'Developing capacity for coastal management in the absence of the government: a case study in the Dominican Republic', *Ocean and Coastal Management*, vol 36, pp47–72

Joubert, A R, Leiman, A, de Klerk, H M, Katau, S and Aggenbach, J C (1997) 'Fynbos vegetation and the supply of water: a comparison of multi-criteria decision analysis and cost–benefit analysis', *Ecological Economics*, vol 22, pp123–140

Kates, R W and Clark, W C (1996) 'Environmental surprise: expecting the unexpected', *Environment*, vol 38 no 2, pp6–11, 28–34

Kelleher, G (ed) (1999) *Guidelines for Marine Protected Areas*, IUCN, Gland

Kenchington, R and Crawford, D (1993) 'On the meaning of integration in coastal zone management', *Ocean and Coastal Management*, vol 21, pp109–127

Kersten, G E (1997) 'Support for group decisions and negotiations: an overview' in Climaco, J (ed) *Multi-Criteria Analysis*, Springer Verlag, Berlin

Kumarsingh, K, Laydoo, R, Chen, J K and Siung-Chang, A M (1998) 'Historic records of phosphorus levels in the reef building coral Montastrea annularis from Tobago, West Indies', *Marine Pollution Bulletin*, vol 36, pp1012–1018

Kusler, J A, Mitsch, W J and Larson, J S (1994) 'Wetlands', *Scientific American*, vol 268 (January), pp50–56

Lapointe, B E and Matzie, W R (1996) 'Effects of stormwater nutrient discharges on eutrophication processes in nearshore waters of the Florida Keys', *Estuaries*, vol 19, pp422–435

Lee, K N (1993) *Compass and Gyroscope: Integrating Science and Politics for the Environment*, Island Press, Washington, DC

Liebman, C B (2000) 'Mediation as parallel seminars: lessons from the student takeover of Columbia University's Hamilton Hall', *Negotiation Journal*, vol 16, pp157–182

Lim, C P, Matsuda, Y and Shigemi, Y (1995) 'Co-management in marine fisheries: the Japanese experience', *Coastal Management*, vol 23, pp195–221

Lock, N (1997) 'Transboundary protected areas between Mexico and Belize', *Coastal Management*, vol 24, pp445–454

Lorenzoni, I, Jordan, A, Hulme, M, Turner, R K and O'Riordan, T (2000) 'A co-evolutionary approach to climate change impact assessment: Part I. Integrating socio-economic and climate change scenarios', *Global Environmental Change*, vol 10, pp57–68

Lubell, M (2000) 'Cognitive conflict and consensus building in the national estuary programme', *American Behavioral Scientist*, vol 44, pp629–648

Lugo, A E, Rogers, C S and Nixon, S W (2000) 'Hurricanes, coral reefs and rainforests: resistance, ruin and recovery in the Caribbean', *Ambio*, vol 29, pp106–114

Luttinger, N (1997) 'Community-based coral reef conservation in the bay islands of Honduras', *Ocean and Coastal Management*, vol 36, pp11–22

Maguire, L A and Boiney, L G (1994) 'Resolving environmental disputes: a framework incorporating decision analysis and dispute resolution techniques', *Journal of Environmental Management*, vol 42, pp31–48

Martinez-Alier, J (2001) 'Ecological conflicts and valuation: mangroves versus shrimps in the late 1990s', *Environment and Planning C: Government and Policy*, vol 19, pp713–728

Matthews, E and Fung, I (1987) 'Methane emissions from natural wetlands: global distribution and environmental characteristics of source', *Global Biogeochemical Cycles*, vol 1, pp61–86

McKean, M (1996) 'Common property regimes as a solution to problems of scale and linkage' in Hanna, S S, Folke, C and Mäler, K-G (eds) *Rights to Nature: Ecological, Economic, Cultural and Political Principles of Institutions for the Environment*, Island Press, Washington, DC

Mikalsen, N H and Jentoft, S (2001) 'From user-groups to stakeholders? the public interest in fisheries management', *Marine Policy*, vol 25, pp281–292

Minnery, J R (1985) *Conflict Management in Urban Planning*, Gower, Brookfield, VT

Mitchell, R K, Agle, B R and Wood, D J (1997) 'Toward a theory of stakeholder identification and salience: defining the principle of who and what really counts', *Academy of Management Review*, vol 22, pp853–886

Moberg, F and Folke, C (1999) 'Ecological goods and services of coral reef ecosystems', *Ecological Economics*, vol 29, pp215–233

Moore, C (1986) *The Mediation Process: Practical Strategies for Resolving Conflict*, Jossey-Bass, San Francisco, CA

Moriki, A, Coccossis, H and Karydis, M (1996) 'Multicriteria evaluation in coastal management', *Journal of Coastal Research*, vol 12, pp171–178

Moscovici, S and Doise, W (1994) *Conflict and Consensus: A General Theory of Collective Decisions*, Sage, London

Myatt-Bell, L B, Scrimshaw, M D, Lester, J N and Potts, J S (2002) 'Public perception of managed realignment: Brancaster West Marsh, North Norfolk, UK', *Marine Policy*, vol 26, pp45–57

Nicholls, R J and Mimura, N (1998) 'Regional issues raised by sea level rise and their policy implications', *Climate Research*, vol 11, pp5–18

Nicholls, R J and Small, C (2002) 'Improved estimates of coastal population and exposure to hazards released', *EOS Transactions*, vol 83, pp301, 305

North, D C (1990) *Institutions, Institutional Change and Economic Performance*, Cambridge University Press, Cambridge

Norton, B, Costanza, R and Bishop, R C (1998) 'The evolution of preferences: why sovereign preferences may not lead to sustainable policies and what to do about it', *Ecological Economics*, vol 24, pp193–211

Nowlis, J S, Roberts, C M, Smith, A H and Siirila, E (1997) 'Human enhanced impacts of a tropical storm on nearshore coral reefs', *Ambio*, vol 26, pp515–521

Nyström, M, Folke, C and Moberg, F (2000) 'Coral reef disturbance and resilience in a human-dominated environment', *Trends in Ecology and Evolution*, vol 15, pp413–417

O'Hara, S U (1996) 'Discursive ethics in ecosystems valuation and environmental policy', *Ecological Economics*, vol 16, pp95–107

Olsen, S B (1993) 'Will integrated coastal management programs be sustainable: the constituency problem', *Ocean and Coastal Management*, vol 21, pp201–225

Olsen, S B and Christie, P (2000) 'What are we learning from tropical coastal management experiences?' *Coastal Management*, vol 28, pp5–18

Olsen, S B, Tobey, J and Hale, L Z (1998) 'A learning-based approach to coastal management', *Ambio*, vol 27, pp611–619

Olsen, S B, Tobey, J and Kerr, M (1997) 'A common framework for learning from ICM experience', *Ocean and Coastal Management*, vol 37, pp155–174

Olson, D L, Mechitov, A I and Moshkovich, H M (2000) 'Multicriteria decision aid techniques: some experimental conclusions', *Research and Practice in Multicriteria Decision Making*, vol 487, pp357–368

Olsson, P and Folke, C (2001) 'Local ecological knowledge and institutional dynamics for ecosystem management: a study of crayfish management in the Lake Racken watershed, Sweden', *Ecosystems*, vol 4, pp85–104

O'Neill, B C, MacKellar, F L and Lutz, W (2001) *Population and Climate Change*, Cambridge University Press, Cambridge

O'Neill, J (2001) 'Representing people, representing nature, representing the world', *Environment and Planning C: Government and Policy*, vol 19, pp483–500

O'Riordan, T (ed) (2000) *Environmental Science for Environmental Management*, second edition, Prentice Hall, Harlow

O'Riordan, T (2001) 'On participatory valuation in shoreline management' in Turner, R K, Bateman, I and Adger, W N (eds) *Economics of Coastal and Water Resources: Valuing Environmental Functions*, Kluwer, Dordrecht

O'Riordan, T and Ward, R (1997) 'Building trust in shoreline management: creating participatory consultation in shoreline management plans', *Land Use Policy*, vol 14, pp257–276

Ostrom, E (1990) *Governing the Commons: The Evolution of Institutions for Collective Action*, Cambridge University Press, Cambridge

Parson, E A and Clark, W C (1995) 'Sustainable development as social learning: theoretical perspectives and practical challenges for the design of a research programme' in Gunderson, L, Holling, C S and Light, S S (eds) *Barriers and Bridges to the Renewal of Ecosystems and Institutions*, Columbia University Press, New York

Pastorok, R A and Bilyard, B G (1985) 'Effects of sewage pollution on coral-reef communities', *Marine Ecology Progress Series*, vol 21, pp175–189

Pattullo, P (1996) *Last Resorts: The Cost of Tourism in the Caribbean*, Cassell, London

Pearce, D W and Markandya, A (1989) *Environmental Policy Benefits: Monetary Valuation*, OECD, Paris

Peña-Torres, J (1997) 'The political economy of fishing regulation: the case of Chile', *Marine Resource Economics*, vol 12, pp239–48.

Petry, F (1990) 'Who is afraid of choices? a proposal for multi-criteria analysis as a tool for decision-making support in development planning', *Journal of International Development*, vol 2, pp209–231

Pezzey, J C V (1997) 'Sustainability constraints versus optimality versus intertemporal concern, and axioms versus data', *Land Economics*, vol 73, pp448–466

Pimbert, M P and Pretty, J N (1994) *Participation, People and the Management of National Parks and Protected Areas: Past Failures and Future Promise*, United Nations Research Institute for Social Development, Geneva

Pinkerton, E W and Weinstein, M (1995) *Fisheries That Work: Sustainability Through Community Based Management*, David Suzuki Foundation, Vancouver

Pondy, L R (1967) 'Organisational conflict: concepts and models', *Administrative Science Quarterly*, vol 12, pp296–320

Powelson, J P (1972) *Institutions of Economic Growth: A Theory of Conflict Management in Developing Countries*, Princeton University Press, Princeton

Pruitt, G D G and Carnevale, P J (1993) *Negotiation in Social Conflict*, Open University Press, Buckingham

Putnam, R D, Leonardi, R and Nanetti, R (1993) *Making Democracy Work: Civic Traditions in Modern Italy*, Princeton University Press, Princeton

Raj, P A (1995) 'Multicriteria methods in river basin planning: a case study', *Water Science Technology*, vol 31, pp261–272

Rajkumar, W and Persad, D (1994) 'Heavy metals and petroleum hydrocarbons in nearshore areas of Tobago, West Indies', *Marine Pollution Bulletin*, vol 28, pp701–703

Rambial, B S (1980) *The Social and Economic Importance of the Caroni Mangrove Swamp Forests*, Paper presented at the 11th Commonwealth Forestry Conference, Trinidad and Tobago, September

Ravnborg, H M and Guerrero, M P (1999) 'Collective action in watershed management: experiences from the Andean hillsides', *Agriculture and Human Values*, vol 16, pp257–266

Rawlins, B G, Ferguson, A J, Chilton, P J, Arthurton, R S and Rees, J G (1998) 'Review of agricultural pollution in the Caribbean with particular emphasis on small island developing states', *Marine Pollution Bulletin*, vol 36, pp658–668

Reaser, J K, Pomerance, R and Thomas, P O (2000) 'Coral bleaching and global climate change: scientific findings and policy recommendations', *Conservation Biology*, vol 14, pp1500–1511

Rijsberman, F (1999) *Conflict Management and Consensus Building for Integrated Coastal Management in Latin America and the Caribbean*, Inter-American Development Bank, Washington DC

Roberts, C M, Bohnsack, J A, Gell, F, Hawkins, J P and Goodridge, R (2001) 'Effects of marine reserves on adjacent fisheries', *Science*, vol 294, pp1920–1923

Roe, M and Benson, J F (2001) 'Planning for conflict resolution: jet-ski use on the Northumberland coast', *Coastal Management*, vol 29, pp19–39

Röling, N G (1994) 'Communication support for sustainable natural resource management', *IDS Bulletin*, vol 25, no 2, pp125–133

Röling, N G and Wagemakers, M A E (eds) (1998) *Facilitating Sustainable Agriculture: Participatory Learning and Adaptive Management in Times of Environmental Uncertainty*, Cambridge University Press, Cambridge

Rönnbäck, P (1999) 'The ecological basis for economic value of seafood production supported by mangrove ecosystems', *Ecological Economics*, vol 29, pp235–252

Rowe, G and Frewer, L J (2000) 'Public participation methods: a framework for evaluation', *Science, Technology and Human Values*, vol 25, pp3–29

Ruddle, K (1998) 'Traditional community-based coastal marine fisheries management in Vietnam', *Ocean and Coastal Management*, vol 40, pp1–22

Ruitenbeek, J and Cartier, C (1999) *Issues in Applied Coral Reef Diversity Valuation: Results for Montego Bay, Jamaica*, Project 682–22, World Bank Research Committee, World Bank, Washington, DC

Ruitenbeek, J and Cartier, C (2001a) 'Prospecting for marine biodiversity: a case study in Montego Bay, Jamaica' in Turner, R K, Bateman, I and Adger, W N (eds)

Economics of Coastal and Water Resources: Valuing Environmental Functions, Kluwer, Dordrecht

Ruitenbeek, J and Cartier, C (2001b) *The Invisible Wand: Adaptive Co-Management as an Emergent Strategy in Complex Bio-economic Systems*, Occasional Paper 34, Centre for International Forestry Research, Bogor, Indonesia

Runge, C F (1984) 'Institutions and the free rider: the assurance problem in collective action', *Journal of Politics*, vol 46, pp152–181

Sagoff, M (1998) 'Aggregation and deliberation in valuing environment public goods: a look beyond contingent pricing', *Ecological Economics*, vol 24, pp213–230

Sandersen, H T and Koester, S (2000) 'Co-management of tropical coastal zones: the case of the Soufrière Marine Management Area, St Lucia, WI', *Coastal Management*, vol 28, pp87–97

Sandler, T (1997) *Global Challenges: An Approach to Environmental, Political and Economic Problems*, Cambridge University Press, Cambridge

Schneider, M, Teske, P and Marschall, M (1997) 'Institutional arrangements and the creation of social capital: the effects of public school choice', *American Political Science Review*, vol 91, pp82–93

Scott, J C (1998) *Seeing Like a State: How Certain Schemes to Improve the Human Condition Have Failed*, Yale University Press, New Haven

Selener, D (1997) *Participatory Action Research and Social Change*, Cornell University Press, Ithaca

Shinn, E A, Smith, G W, Prospero, J M, Betzer, P, Hayes, M L, Garrison, V and Barber, R T (2000) 'African dust and the demise of Caribbean coral reefs', *Geophysical Research Letters*, vol 27, pp3029–3032

Singleton, S (2000) 'Co-operation or capture? the paradox of co-management and community participation in natural resource management and environmental policy-making', *Environmental Politics*, vol 9, no 2, pp1–21

Slocombe, D S (1993) 'Environmental planning, ecosystem science, and ecosystem approaches for integrating environment and development', *Environmental Management*, vol 17, pp289–303

Slovic, P (2000) 'Perceived risk, trust, and democracy' in Connolly, T, Arkes, H R and Hammond, K R (eds) *Judgement and Decision Making: An Interdisciplinary Reader*, Cambridge University Press, Cambridge

Sorensen, J (1997) 'National and international efforts at integrated coastal management: definitions, achievements and lessons', *Coastal Management*, vol 25, pp3–41

Souter, D W and Linden, O (2000) 'The health and future of coral reef systems', *Ocean and Coastal Management*, vol 43, pp657–688

Spash, C L (2001) Special theme issue on participation, representation and deliberation in environmental policy: *Environment and Planning C: Government and Policy*, vol 19, no 4

Steins, N A and Edwards, V M (1998) 'Harbour resource management in Cowes, Isle of Wight: an analytical framework for multiple-use decision-making', *Journal of Environmental Management*, vol 54, pp67–81

Steins, N A and Edwards, V M (1999) 'Collective action in common pool resource management: the contribution of social constructivist perspectives to existing theory', *Society and Natural Resources*, vol 12, pp539–557

Stewart, T J and Scott, L (1995) 'A scenario-based framework for multicriteria decision analysis in water resources planning', *Water Resources Research*, vol 31, pp2835–2843

Streeten, P (1993) 'The special problems of small countries', *World Development*, vol 21, pp197–202

Sudara, S (1999) 'Who and what is to be involved in successful coastal zone management: a Thailand example', *Ocean and Coastal Management*, vol 42, pp39–47

Sumaila, A R, Guenette, S, Alder, J, Pollard, D and Chuenpagdee, R (1999) *Marine Protected Areas and Managing Fished Ecosystems*, Report 4, Chr Michelsen Institute, Bergen, Norway

Swallow, B M and Bromley, D W (1995) 'Institutions, governance and incentives in common property regimes for African rangelands', *Environmental and Resource Economics*, vol 6, pp99–118

Tacconi, L (1997) 'Property rights and participatory biodiversity conservation: lessons from Malekula Island, Vanuatu', *Land Use Policy*, vol 14, pp151–161

Taylor, M (1996) 'Good government: on hierarchy, social capital, and the limitations of rational choice theory', *Journal of Political Philosophy*, vol 4, pp1–28.

Taylor, M (1998) 'Governing natural resources', *Society and Natural Resources*, vol 11, pp251–258.

Thorburn, C C (2000) 'Changing customary marine resource management practice and institutions: the case of Sasi Lola in the Kei Islands, Indonesia', *World Development*, vol 28, pp1461–1479

Ticco, P C (1995) 'The use of marine protected areas to preserve and enhance marine biological diversity: a case study approach', *Coastal Management*, vol 23, pp309–314

Tomascik, T and Sander, F (1985) 'Effects of eutrophication on reef-building corals 1: growth rate of the reef-building coral *Montastrea annularis*', *Marine Biology*, vol 87, pp143–155

Tompkins, E, Adger, W N and Brown, K (2002) 'Institutional networks as components of integrated and inclusive coastal zone management in Trinidad and Tobago', *Environment and Planning A*, vol 34, pp1095–1111

Tonn, B, English, M and Travis, C (2000) 'A framework for understanding and improving environmental decision making', *Journal of Environmental Planning and Management*, vol 43, pp163–183

Turner, R K (2000) 'Integrating natural and socio-economic science in coastal management', *Journal of Marine Systems*, vol 25, pp447–460

Turner, R K, Subak, S and Adger, W N (1996) 'Pressures, trends and impacts in coastal zones: interactions between socio-economic and natural systems', *Environmental Management*, vol 20, pp159–173

Turner, R K, Georgiou, S, Gren, I-M, Wulff, F, Barrett, S, Soderqvist, T, Bateman, I J, Folke, C, Langaas, S, Zylicz, T, Mäler, K-G and Markowska, A (1999) 'Managing nutrient fluxes and pollution in the Baltic: an interdisciplinary simulation study.' *Ecological Economics*, vol 30, pp333–352

Turner, R K, Bateman, I and Adger, W N (eds) (2001) *Economics of Coastal and Water Resources: Valuing Environmental Functions*, Kluwer, Dordrecht

Van Ginkel, R (1996) 'The abundant sea and her fates: texelian oystermen and the marine commons, 1700 to 1932', *Comparative Studies in Society and History*, vol 38, pp218–242

Van Ginkel, R (1999) 'Contextualising marine resource use: a case from The Netherlands', *Journal of Environmental Policy and Planning*, vol 1, pp223–233

Vatn, A (2001) 'Environmental resources, property regimes and efficiency', *Environment and Planning C: Government and Policy*, vol 19, pp665–680

Venter, A K and Breen, C M (1998) 'Partnership forum framework: participative framework for protected area outreach', *Environmental Management*, vol 22, pp803–815

Wade, R (1988) *Village Republics: Economic Conditions for Collective Action in South India*, Cambridge University Press, Cambridge

Walters, J S (1994) 'Coastal common property regimes in Southeast Asia' in Borgese, E M, Ginsburg, N and Morgan, J R (eds) *Ocean Yearbook 11*, University of Chicago Press, Chicago

Warner, M (2000) *Conflict Management in Community-Based Natural Resource Projects: Experiences from Fiji and Papua New Guinea*, Working Paper 135, Overseas Development Institute, London

Weaver, D B (1998) 'Peripheries of the periphery: tourism in Tobago and Barbuda', *Annals of Tourism Research*, vol 25, pp292–313

Westmacott, S, Teleki, K, Wells, S and West, J M (2000) *Management of Bleached and Severely Damaged Coral Reefs*, IUCN, Gland, Switzerland

White, A T, Hale, L Z, Renard, Y and Cortesi, L (1994) *Collaborative and Community-based Management of Coral Reefs: Lessons from Experience*, Kumarian Press, Hartford, CT

Wilkinson, C (ed) (2000) *Status of Coral Reefs of the World: 2000*, Australian Institute of Marine Science, Cape Ferguson, Australia

Woodley, D J (1997) 'CARICOMP monitoring of coral reefs in the Caribbean', *Proceedings of the Eighth International Coral Reefs Symposium*, vol 1, pp651–656

Woolcock, M and Narayan, D (2000) 'Social capital: implications for development theory, research and policy', *World Bank Research Observer*, vol 15, pp225–249

WRI (World Resources Institute) (2001) 'Data on world fisheries', World Resources Institute, Washington, DC at www.wri.org

WWF International (1998) *Marine Protected Areas. WWF's Role in Their Future Development*, Discussion Paper, WWF International, Gland, Switzerland

Index

Integration 121–122
  defined 20
Interdisciplinary approaches 2, 20, 54,
  121
Interests (see Stakeholder interests)
Interventions in conflict 114
Interviews 74, 75, 100, 105, 124

Knowledge 21, 57, 78, 108, 109, 113
  control of 136
  lay 29, 52, 57, 77, 99, 114
  sharing 4, 36, 49, 114, 138

Lakes 7, 30
Land use 64, 94
Latent stakeholders 70, 71, 72
Laws (see legal framework)
Learning 54, 61, 79, 120, 137
  social learning 49–50, 51, 77, 109, 119,
  121, 127, 137
  institutional 3, 4, 9, 79
  political learning 49, 50, 57
Learning-based approaches 18, 21, 119,
  140
Legal frameworks 27–28, 38, 46, 122,
  123, 124, 125, 135
  fisheries 32
  marine environmental laws 27
  umbrella regulations 64
  UN Law of the Sea 28, 145
Legitimacy 2, 14, 19, 41, 50, 57, 61, 67,
  70, 71, 78, 81
Livelihoods 2, 4, 14, 22, 45, 104, 64, 72,
  92, 93

Maldives 11, 12, 13, 14
Management (see Community based
  resource management, Integrated
  coastal zone management,
  Integrated conservation and
  development, Participatory resource
  management, Successful
  management, and Traditional
  resource management)
Mangroves 4, 56, 94, 95, 96, 132
Marine protected areas 19, 20, 32–33, 34,
  35, 65, 108, 123, 125
  objectives of 18, 32
  first recorded 19
  legislated 27
  problems associated with 64

Marshes 7
MCA (see Multi-criteria analysis)
Measurability 88
Measurable indicators 87, 88, 92, 95, 96,
  97
Mexico 4, 35, 66
MPAs (see Marine protected areas)
Multi-criteria analysis 62, 78, 79, 80–81,
  96–99, 104–107, 118–119
Multi-criteria mapping 58
Multiple use resources 18, 24, 32, 33, 41,
  62, 64, 65, 78

Netherlands 3, 10, 47
Negotiating 2, 83, 112, 115, 139
  platforms 129
Networks 49–52, 59, 119, 123, 126, 137,
  139
  spaces of dependence and engagement
  51, 128
New Zealand 32, 48
Nitrates 94, 95, 97, 98
Norfolk, UK (see UK)
Norway 3, 48, 70–71
Nutrients 5, 6, 9, 15, 16, 24, 30, 34, 35,
  64, 89, 94

Open ended surveys 90, 91
Operational arrangements 51, 52, 61,
  124, 125
Organizational structures 26, 33, 74, 122,
  123, 124, 125, 126

Participation 57, 74, 88, 100, 117, 120,
  131
  benefits of 18, 19, 108, 113
  critical elements of 81
  critiques of 48–49, 131, 132
  forms of 54, 56
  stakeholders and 52–55
Participatory resource management 45,
  51, 55, 122, 126, 132, 133
  constraints to 124
  institutions for 51–52, 138
  in the USA 134
  preconditions for successful 134, 135,
  137, 138
Participatory rural appraisal 58
Pile drivers 132
Political will 46, 47, 85, 114, 122
Pollution 55